Centre for Educational Research and Innovation

Trends Shaping Education

2008 Edition

OECD

ORGANISATION FOR ECONOMIC CO-OPERATION AND DEVELOPMENT

The OECD is a unique forum where the governments of 30 democracies work together to address the economic, social and environmental challenges of globalisation. The OECD is also at the forefront of efforts to understand and to help governments respond to new developments and concerns, such as corporate governance, the information economy and the challenges of an ageing population. The Organisation provides a setting where governments can compare policy experiences, seek answers to common problems, identify good practice and work to co-ordinate domestic and international policies.

The OECD member countries are: Australia, Austria, Belgium, Canada, the Czech Republic, Denmark, Finland, France, Germany, Greece, Hungary, Iceland, Ireland, Italy, Japan, Korea, Luxembourg, Mexico, the Netherlands, New Zealand, Norway, Poland, Portugal, the Slovak Republic, Spain, Sweden, Switzerland, Turkey, the United Kingdom and the United States. The Commission of the European Communities takes part in the work of the OECD.

OECD Publishing disseminates widely the results of the Organisation's statistics gathering and research on economic, social and environmental issues, as well as the conventions, guidelines and standards agreed by its members.

This work is published on the responsibility of the Secretary-General of the OECD. The opinions expressed and arguments employed herein do not necessarily reflect the official views of the Organisation or of the governments of its member countries.

Also available in French under the title:
Les grandes mutations qui transforment l'éducation – Édition 2008

Foreword

This book is designed to support long-term strategic thinking in education. It provides an overview of trends in the context of education and raises pertinent questions about their impact on education. This compilation relies mainly, but not exclusively, on OECD sources. It gives, as far as possible, robust international evidence of the trends.

This book fills an important need: decision makers and practitioners in education often have only anecdotal or local information on the major changes that play out in their context; too often they do not have solid facts in front of them, especially about trends.

Within the OECD Centre for Educational Research and Innovation (CERI), this publication was written by David Istance and Henno Theisens, with Petra Packalen, Francisco Benavides, Kristina Kaihari-Salminen and Paula Mattila making substantial contribution. Delphine Grandrieux prepared it for publication.

TABLE OF CONTENTS

LIST OF FIGURES

TRENDS SHAPING EDUCATION – ISBN 978-92-64-04661-0 – © OECD 2008

Introduction

What does it mean for education that our societies are ageing? What does it mean that the Internet is playing an ever larger role in our lives? Does it matter for schools that populations are increasingly overweight?

This book is designed to help thinking about major developments that are affecting the future of education and setting challenges for schools. It does not give conclusive answers: it is not an analytical report nor is it a statistical compendium, and it is certainly not a statement of OECD policy on these different developments. It is instead:

- A stimulus for thinking about trends influencing education – while the trends are robust, the questions raised for education are illustrative and suggestive.

- An invitation for users to look further and to add to this basic coverage examples of trends from their own countries or regions.

Using trends is not straightforward. Opinions differ on historical developments and which ones are most important. Even when there is agreement on the past, the future will often not turn out to be a smooth continuation of past patterns. Moreover, emerging trends barely visible or noticed at the present time may become critically important in the future. To help the reader use this resource, this first section discusses how trends may be addressed and interpreted.

FOR WHOM IS THIS TOOL RELEVANT?

We think that this tool will be relevant for everyone active in the field of education. We have tried to avoid jargon and technical terminology and the format has been chosen to make complex data accessible.

- *Policy makers, officials, advisors and policy analysts* may use it as a source of robust trends to build on in thinking through the long-term possibilities for education and what the trends might mean for school policies.

- *School and local leaders and other stakeholders* who increasingly need to make long-term, strategic plans or are being consulted on such decisions may use the tool to inform the choices they face.

- *Teacher educators* may use it as material for programmes aimed at student and practising teachers and at school leaders to help them consider their futures and professional practice.

- *Teachers* can use it as an aid for professional development and as a starting point for reflection on practice and curriculum issues.

There are others who may find this selection of trends equally stimulating. The choice of trends and the treatment given to them in the text, however, are designed especially for those working in the educational field and specifically those with a particular interest in school-age learning.

WHY THESE TRENDS?

This resource contains 26 major topics each illustrated by 2 figures. While all the trends included are relevant to education, not all relevant trends are in this resource – it is necessarily highly selective. As well as relevance for education, the criterion for selection has been the presence of international through-time evidence. This inevitably biases its coverage towards the economic, social, environmental, demographic and educational fields where measurements have been in place long enough to give a picture of developments over time. Some of the factors importantly shaping education are highly subjective and cultural in content, making them difficult to pin down at any one time, let alone over time, and these are not covered.

The focus is primarily on OECD countries, though where they are available, broader global data are used. The different sources mean that there are no single time frames: in some cases the trends are charted over a short decade or so; in some others, very long-term trends are available.

We therefore stress that this resource is a stimulus to further thinking, not a compendium of all the major trends relevant to the future of schooling.

WHY THIS FORMAT AND STRUCTURE?

The trends have been grouped into nine broad themes, each with a short introduction as well as a list of publications for further reference. Each theme consists of two, three or four topics or sets of trends, each topic presented in two-page format. Each of these starts with a short introduction, followed by two figures and accompanying text. We conclude each topic with illustrative questions about education that the trends give rise to in order to stimulate reflection and further questions. There is no one best way to order these broad themes, but we think that the structure chosen provides a helpful introduction:

- First, there are major demographic trends. These concern the OECD countries and lead on to global developments not just of population levels and movements but living conditions and the environment.

- Second, there are economic trends relating both to the nature of economies and to the kinds of work and jobs people do.

- Third, we present themes related to the digital (and learning) society in which we live, in which education makes its own important contribution.

- Fourth, there are the political and social factors to do with the role of the state, the social environment and families, and trends concerning sustainability.

HOW TO USE THIS RESOURCE

The future is inherently unpredictable. Yet, everyone – including policy makers and managers in education – needs to make plans and take the future into account. Looking at trends informs our ideas about what might happen through better understanding of what is changing in education's environment.

When studying trends we are studying the past and there are no guarantees that the future will see past developments continue, let alone continue smoothly. We can sometimes be just plain wrong:

TRENDS SHAPING EDUCATION – ISBN 978-92-64-04661-0 – © OECD 2008

"Stocks have reached what looks like a permanently high plateau." (Irving Fisher, Professor of Economics, Yale University, just before the 1929 Wall St. Crash)

Nor is it guaranteed that the trends that were important in the past or seem so now will remain influential in the future; emerging trends barely visible at the moment may become of central importance in the future. When aircraft were just beginning to become operational, the military leader who was to become Commander-in-Chief during WWI declared:

"Airplanes are interesting toys but of no military value." (Maréchal Ferdinand Foch, École Supérieure de Guerre)

This book is thus a starting point and not conclusive about what is setting directions for the future. The following questions are useful when thinking about trends.

WHICH TRENDS ARE RELEVANT?

Is this trend relevant in this specific context?

Trends may differ both in size and direction in different countries, regions, districts or even schools. Ageing populations, for example, may be a bigger problem in rural than in urban areas or concentrated in certain parts of the country or districts in a city. International trends may have different impacts in different places: rising sea levels are potentially disastrous for Bangladesh but not for Nepal.

Are there other trends to take into account?

The trends in this resource are certainly not the only relevant ones and not all of them apply equally in each location or context. There may be other, perhaps local, trends that will be just as important to consider. Different places face different challenges: some, for instance, are declining and de-populating while other areas even in the same country are booming and attracting new people. Users will need to think of what are the important trends for their purpose.

HOW IMPORTANT ARE THESE TRENDS?

How predictable is this trend?

Trends differ as to how far their continuation is predictable. Some trends – for instance, to do with population growth or environment – lend themselves more easily to long-term planning. Others are less predictable, such as those to do with youth culture or international conflict. For these, making scenarios of what would happen if a particular trend would develop in a certain way may well be more appropriate than extrapolation.

What is the pace of this trend?

Some trends develop slowly (global temperatures went up around 0.74 °C in the last 100 years) while other trends are more dynamic (international trade in services quadrupled in less than twenty years). Trends with a slow pace are easier to deal with in the sense that they allow for more time to think about what they mean and how to respond.

What is the impact of the trend?

Climate change may be slow but its potential impact is enormous, possibly threatening life on our planet. Other trends like changing fashion may be more rapid, but have less impact on education. Generally, the more impact the trend has, the more important it is to anticipate it.

HOW CAN WE DEAL WITH THESE TRENDS?

Can we predict?

When trends are predictable, long-term planning is greatly facilitated. With demographic change fairly predictable and all children going into primary education, the capacity needed in primary education in, say, 10 years time is open to calculation.

Can we influence?

If trends are not predictable it may still be possible to influence them. Universities have great difficulty in predicting the number of students who will choose a certain study programme. However, they can attempt to influence the numbers of students applying through advertising campaigns.

Can we react?

If both predicting and influencing are impossible, creating the flexibility to be able to react after events occur may be the best option. For example, someone starting a business who does not know how it will take off is better advised to lease offices than buy them.

TRENDS SHAPING EDUCATION – ISBN 978-92-64-04661-0 – © OECD 2008

ISBN 978-92-64-04661-0
Trends Shaping Education
© OECD 2008

Chapter 1

Ageing OECD Societies

– FEWER CHILDREN
– LIVING LONGER
– CHANGING AGE STRUCTURES

The notion of "ageing societies" covers a major set of trends about populations which include, but go well beyond, the fact that people now live longer. It is equally about numbers of children and babies, and what goes on within families. These big trends have profound and direct impacts on schools, and we focus on three related aspects:

- *There are fewer and fewer children being born in OECD societies.*

- *We are living longer.*

- *There is a new shape to the population distribution as numbers in the different age groups change.*

We can show these trends accurately to the present day but forecasting the future is altogether more difficult. For example, many more people may die young than could have been expected at any given time (through wars or a pandemic like HIV/AIDS). Behaviour can shift unpredictably and with it long-term historical trends, such as the half of child-bearing couples worldwide who now use contraception which would have been difficult to predict as recently as the 1960s, when just 1 in 10 did so.

Nevertheless, we include the most authoritative available population forecasts to gain a picture of the long-term changes taking place.

FEWER CHILDREN

There have been rapid changes in the number of children being born, with births falling dramatically. Families are smaller, women tend to be older when they have children, and more do not have children at all. Education is part of the story, with higher levels of education tending to be associated with fewer children. The number of children born in OECD countries is now so low that the long-term prospect is of population decline, despite the fact that we are living longer as discussed next. On average 2.1 children per woman should be born in a country for there to be long-term population stability: when it is significantly lower than this the population falls. By the beginning of the 21st century, only two OECD countries – Mexico and Turkey – were still above the 2.1 line. This is in sharp contrast with many developing countries where fertility levels remain high.

Figure 1.1. **Birth rates well down on the 1960s**
Total fertility rates: children per woman aged 15-49, 1960, 1980 and 2003

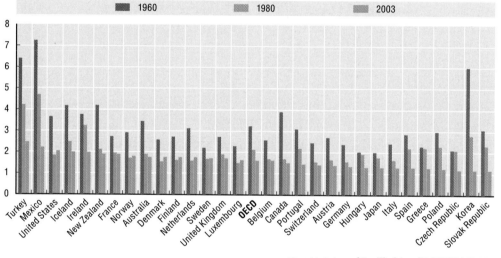

StatLink 📊 http://dx.doi.org/10.1787/403484727486

Source: OECD (2005), *Health at a Glance.*

This figure shows two key aspects about birth rates. One is change over the approximately 40 years since 1960. The other is the relative position of the different OECD countries, ordered left to right from those with highest current birth rates to those with the lowest. We see just how significant has been the drop in birth rates. The OECD average was over 3 births per woman aged 15-49 years in 1960 which has been cut in half in only 45 years. For some countries, the fall in the number of children being born has been truly dramatic – such as Korea, which has gone from one of the highest fertility rates of the 30 countries to one of the lowest.

Another pattern which stands out is how similar the birth rates have now become across most countries, with around two-thirds of them belonging in the narrow range 1.3 to 1.8 births for each woman aged 15-49. Compare this with the differences at the start of the 1960s, when some countries (Japan, Hungary, the Czech Republic) already had low birth rates of around 2 while others (Korea, Mexico, Turkey, Iceland, New Zealand) were more than twice as high. Some might be surprised to see Nordic countries to the left of the figure – higher fertility – and Southern European ones with lower fertility, to the right.

The second figure showing the age of mothers when they have their first child reinforces the picture. It underscores the extent of recent change in social behaviour. In 1970, in only 3 of the 16 countries in the figure was the average age for starting motherhood 25 years or more; by 2004, in none of them was it less than 25. The mothers' age on having their first child now approaches 28 years for the 16 countries whereas in 1970 it was 24 years.

Figure 1.2. **Starting parenthood later**

Average age when mothers have their first child in a number of OECD countries

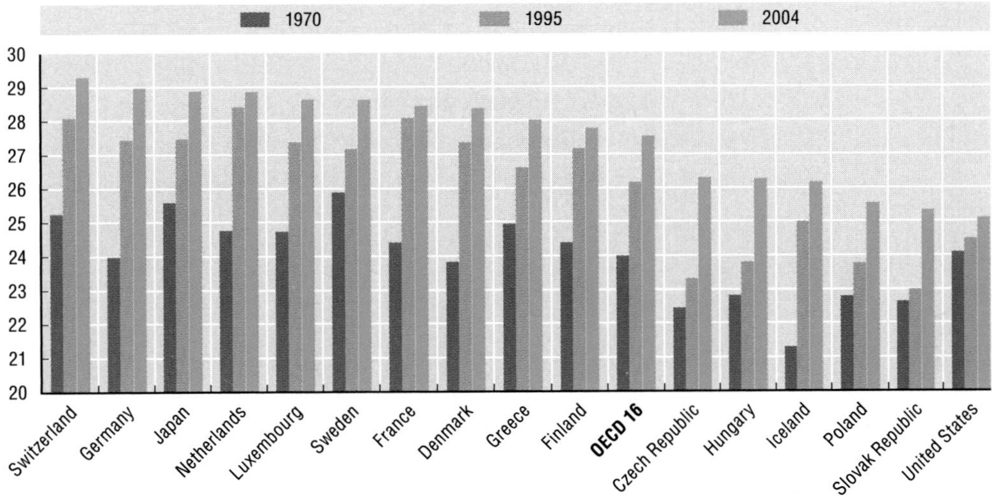

StatLink ▄▄▄▄ http://dx.doi.org/10.1787/403553827574

Source: OECD (2006), Society at a Glance.

And education?

- School rolls fall as numbers of young people fall. For some countries that have been experiencing severe teacher shortages this may be a welcome trend. But some countries or regions face difficult questions: how to deal with emptying and closing schools, and the possible reduction in school choices in some communities?

- Falling enrolments present opportunities, not just problems. Is the opportunity being seized to make resources go further for each student and to engage in innovation that would be impossible if schools were completely full? What about new school designs and buildings?

- What does it mean for young people coming into education to have older parents and fewer, often no, brothers and sisters? How does it change the way in which they experience (school) life and how will schools need to respond to this profound change?

LIVING LONGER

Never before have people lived longer than today and the gains in the last century have been particularly remarkable. Life expectancy has increased not just in the OECD area but in many other countries, too. The trend to live longer is not without exceptions as life expectancy has gone down in recent years in some central and eastern European countries and parts of sub-Saharan Africa. Women live longer than men in OECD countries and, while life expectancy is steadily going up for both, the gap is not closing. The extent of longevity after the conventional retirement age raises profound questions about the nature of this phase of our lives and the sustainability of pensions practice. It also invites reflection about the role of education which so often is seen as primarily for young people.

Figure 1.3. **People live longer**

Year of life expectancy at birth (average for both sexes)

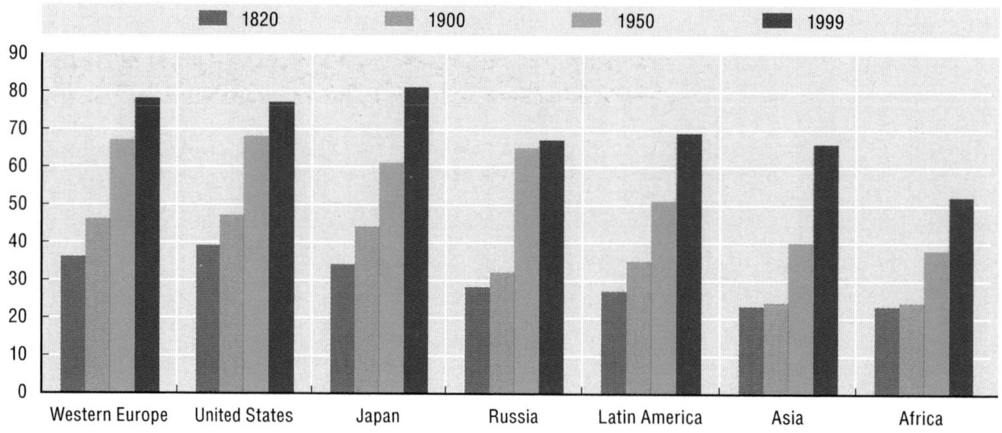

StatLink ⬛⬛⬛ http://dx.doi.org/10.1787/403564674676

Source: OECD (2003), *The World Economy: Historical Statistics.*

Life expectancy from 1820 to the end of the 20th century had more than doubled everywhere in the world. The largest increases in life expectancy has been realised in the past 100 years, associated with factors such as improved living conditions, hygiene and preventive health care.

There are still huge differences within the global average – with people in Africa having an average life expectancy that is more than 25 years less than in Western Europe, the United States, and Japan. There have been only very small increases in life expectancy in Russia in the last 50 years, a reflection of the unhealthy lifestyles particularly of men (especially smoking and alcohol consumption). The last 20 years have been even more dramatic for those African countries which have been most severely affected by HIV/AIDS.

Almost everywhere in the world women live longer than men. The next figure shows that in OECD countries, a woman reaching age 65 could expect on average to live to over 80 in 1970 (65+15), while for men in 1970 the OECD average was under 78. Life expectancy after retirement age goes up steadily in the 1980s and 1990s for both men and women and for women is approaching the 85-year mark (65+20). But men, though living longer, are not closing this gap with women.

Living longer has profound consequences. Not only does it affect the population age structure of our societies, with relatively more people over 65 than ever before. It also affects the sustainability of social policies: the retirement age was set at mid-sixties, for example, when on average people expected to live for only a few years afterwards. Now, men can expect to live for another 16 years on average and women nearly 20. Longer life also affects the meaning of old age: it means enjoying potentially many more healthy years, but also more of us becoming very elderly with possible losses in the quality of life.

Figure 1.4. **Longer lives after retirement age**
Average additional life expectancy of 65-year-old men and women in OECD countries

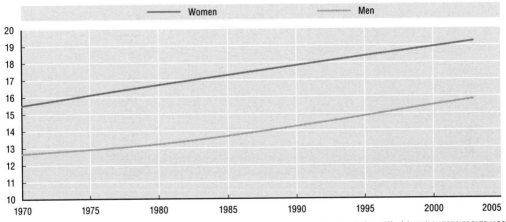

StatLink ⫘ http://dx.doi.org/10.1787/403617841587

Note: The average excludes: Iceland, Korea, Spain and Switzerland.
Source: OECD (2005), *OECD Health Data.*

And education?

- When we expect schooling to prepare young people "for life", that means something very different if average life expectancy is 80 to 90 years than when it is only to 50 to 60 years. Do our "long-life" societies call for re-thinking what education should equip young people with?

- What role should the school system be playing in meeting the learning and cultural needs of the many older members of the population? Is it doing enough?

- A lot of older people will be active, mentally and physically, much longer. But such a growth in numbers of elderly people also means many more of us are frail and in need of care, all of which has to be paid for. How will this affect the school sector? What new pressures will there be on resources?

CHANGING AGE STRUCTURES

The combined effect of living longer and fewer children is transforming population structures. Such structures that even 50 years ago were like pyramids, with a broad base of young age groups and a small top of older people, are being transformed into a "top heavy" shape with a narrower base, a bulging middle moving steadily up, and a long, tapering top. "Dependency ratios" compare the size of the age groups often characterised by financial independence with those who may well be dependent, such as children or the elderly. Very significant increases in the ratios of the 65+ age group can be expected, compared with the middle 15-64 year-olds, with potentially far-reaching consequences on resources available for education.

Figure 1.5. **From "bottom-heavy" to "top-heavy" age structures**

Age structure in more developed regions with millions of people per age bracket (i.e. Europe, plus Northern America, Australia, New Zealand and Japan) in 1950 and 2050

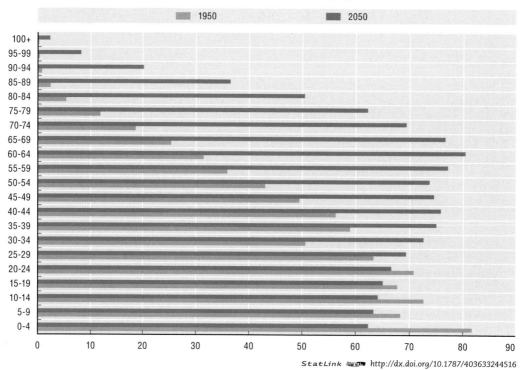

StatLink ⫘ *http://dx.doi.org/10.1787/403633244516*

Source: United Nations (2006), World Population Prospects: The 2006 Revision, online version, *http://esa.un.org/unpp/index.asp?panel=2*, accessed June 2007.

In Europe and other developed regions, both the actual numbers of children and their share in the total population are decreasing while conversely the older age groups are increasing across the board. In the more developed countries, it is expected that in 2050 there will be more people aged 70 to 74 than in any of the 5-year age bands up to the age of 29. There will even be around as many 75-79 year-olds as 0 to 5-year-olds.

The next figure looks at "dependency ratios". These compare the proportions in age groups often characterised by financial independence with those in age groups who may well be dependent, such as children or the elderly. The "old-age dependency ratio" compares the share of the 65+ age group with the population broadly of "working age" (15 to 64). (It should be stressed that these indicators recognise that many in the 65+ age

TRENDS SHAPING EDUCATION – ISBN 978-92-64-04661-0 – © OECD 2008

group are not "dependent" just as many aged 15-64 are not in paid employment, either.) When the age structure is "bottom-heavy", the key dependency ratios concern children and young people, whereas with the move to the "top-heavy" pattern the focus is shifting increasingly to the older population.

Looking out from 2000 to 2050 across the OECD, numbers of people aged 65+ compared with the 15-64 year-olds are foreseen to more than double. Instead of there being only one 65+ year-old to five 15-64 year-olds in 2000 it is expected that this ratio will fall to nearly one to two (47%) by 2050. The share of older to younger adults is expected to be especially high in the Mediterranean countries of Greece, Italy and Spain, and in Japan at around two in the 65+ bracket for every three 15-64 year-olds. Some of the highest rates of change in this regard will be in countries like Mexico and Turkey with the lowest shares of older people at present.

Figure 1.6. **The "old age dependency ratio" set to double by 2050**

Population aged 65 and over relative to the population of 15-64 in 2000 and 2050

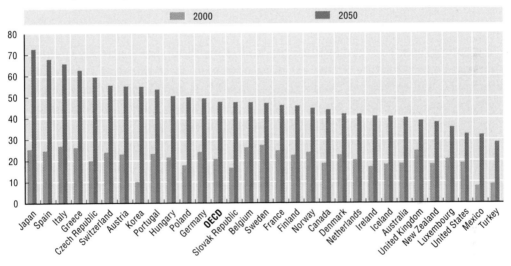

StatLink http://dx.doi.org/10.1787/403710262251

Source: OECD (2006), Society at a Glance.

And education?

- The smaller age groups coming to leave education and enter the labour market will not replace the retiring baby-boom generation. Will our current understanding of terms like "school-leaving age", "working age" and "retirement age" come under pressure to change and towards what?

- A common question to ask about rising older "dependency" ratios is whether public expenditure will rocket for healthcare and pensions, leaving less for education for the young. Another is: "who will pay taxes when numbers fall in the working age groups?"

- Can we continue with ever-lengthening periods of time spent by young people in initial education? Do we need more flexible, less linear models which get young people sooner out of education, and, if so, what guarantees to return to education later in life are needed?

FIND OUT MORE

OECD publications used

- OECD (2003), *The World Economy: Historical Statistics*, OECD Publishing, Paris.
- OECD (2005), *Health at a Glance*, 2005 Edition, OECD Publishing, Paris.
- OECD (2006), *Society at a Glance*, 2006 Edition, OECD Publishing, Paris.
- OECD (2006), *Live Longer, Work Longer*, OECD Publishing, Paris.

Relevant websites

- United Nations, World Population Prospects: The 2006 Revision, online version, *http://esa.un.org/unpp/index.asp?panel=2*, accessed June 2007.

Further literature

- OECD (2005), *Babies and Bosses*, OECD Publishing, Paris.

Definitions and measurement

- *Total fertility rates*: The total fertility rate is not something that is actually counted. It is not based on the fertility of any real group of women, since this would involve waiting until they had completed childbearing. Instead it is calculated by imagining that a woman would go through her entire fertile life (15 to 49), where her fertility for each age is based on the current fertility for that specific age group.

- *Life expectancy*: Life expectancy is the average number of years a human has before death, conventionally calculated from the time of birth (but also can be calculated from any specified age). Calculating this starts with taking the current death rate for people of each age, which also gives one the probability to survive at each age (*e.g.* if 20% of the 90-year-olds die before they turn 91, probability to survive at that age is 80%). The life expectancy is then calculated by adding up these probabilities to survive. This is the expected number of complete years lived.

ISBN 978-92-64-04661-0
Trends Shaping Education
© OECD 2008

Chapter 2

Global Challenges

– OUR CROWDED PLANET

– INTERNATIONAL DIVIDES OF AFFLUENCE AND POVERTY

– POPULATIONS ON THE MOVE

– GLOBAL ENVIRONMENTAL CHALLENGES

What takes place in other parts of the planet has profound consequences for our own societies and vice versa – we live in a global world.

In this section, we look at four main issues:

- *Our crowded planet.*
- *Widening divides between affluent and poor countries.*
- *More migration, more diversity.*
- *Global environmental challenges.*

The demographics of populations in the more affluent and ageing OECD countries, which are no longer experiencing population growth, are put into sharp relief when compared with the very different trends experienced in many other parts of the world.

There are stark and growing inequalities in living standards across the world. These inequalities are key factors in migration which has become such an important aspect of the contemporary world. With populations on the move, they bring far-reaching consequences for the mix of peoples and cultures of the countries to which they go. The diversity is experienced very directly by our education systems.

Our interdependence with every other part of the planet is nowhere more striking than with regards to the environment, and here we are facing some of our most intractable long-term problems.

OUR CROWDED PLANET

We live on a very crowded planet. More and more people are being born and many of us are living longer. At the same time the world is growing smaller, with the sense of distance which separates countries and communities shrinking due to the speed of international travel and communications. Based on the current estimates of UN demographers, the present world population of 6.4 billion is forecast to grow to 8.9 billion by 2050. While the richer OECD countries experience ageing and declining numbers, populations continue to grow in many other places. The demographic challenges of an ageing society for education systems described above are not experienced by most of the rest of the world.

Figure 2.1. **Population stagnation in OECD countries, growth elsewhere**

Population growth worldwide and in more and less developed countries (in billions)

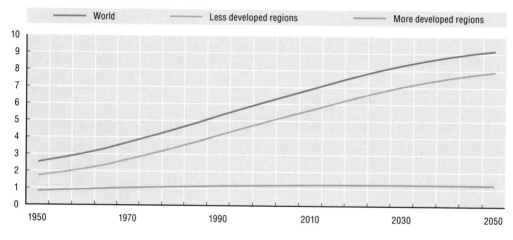

StatLink ⬛ *http://dx.doi.org/10.1787/403711567004*

Note: More developed regions are all regions of Europe plus Northern America, Australia/New Zealand and Japan, less developed regions are defined as the rest of the world.

Source: United Nations (2006), World Population Prospects: The 2006 Revision, online version, *http://esa.un.org/unpp/index.asp?panel=2*, accessed June 2007.

The first figure shows the very wide, and growing, differences between the richer and poorer parts of the world. The flat line at the bottom represents numbers in more affluent countries which, after the baby booms of the 1950s and 1960s, hardly change. This is in very marked contrast to the less developed countries, where numbers have already grown enormously and look set to continue to do so. The world population more than doubled in the second half of the 20th century; it is anticipated to rise by a further 3 billion in the next fifty years. If already there are severe pressures building up because of the very different conditions of life in the rich and poor parts of the world, such forecasts lead us to expect that these pressures will get even stronger in years to come.

The same UN sources also chart the long-term trend to urbanisation as more and more of us live in cities and suburban environments, with relatively high densities of population (this provides only an approximate picture as the United Nations relies on national definitions of "urban"). This trend to urbanisation is happening in both the rich and poor countries of the world, with the difference between the two steadily closing over

TRENDS SHAPING EDUCATION – ISBN 978-92-64-04661-0 – © OECD 2008

the past 20-30 years. The trend often creates problems, especially in the less developed countries, of creaking infrastructure in the cities and impoverished services in the depopulated countryside.

Towns and cities often enjoy opportunities unavailable in rural areas; job opportunities are, after all, the "pull" factor that makes so many decide to move. They mean larger numbers living closer together. But urbanisation also means disruption to traditional ties and norms – progress in some circumstances, alienation and isolation in others. In some OECD countries, this is leading to a partial revival of rural areas as people embrace tele-working and look for alternatives to crowded town life.

Figure 2.2. **More people live in urban environments**

Percentage of people living in areas classified as urban by national authorities

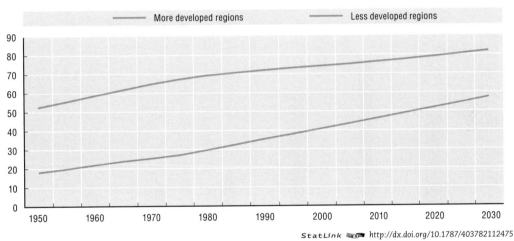

StatLink ▒▒▒ http://dx.doi.org/10.1787/403782112475

Source: United Nations (2006), World Population Prospects: The 2006 Revision, online version, *http://esa.un.org/unpp/index.asp?panel=2*, accessed June 2007.

And education?

- Growing world populations have very clear resource implication. Is the Millennium Goal of primary education for all realistic, given that the world population is set to rise by a further 3 billion up to the mid-21st century?

- Urbanisation at very rapid rates places services, including education, under strain. How also to cope with the problems of overcrowding and overstretched infrastructures in the urban areas affected? How to deal with declining populations, loss of dynamism, and emptying schools in the countryside?

- Can the school act as a "social anchor" for rapidly-expanding urban populations experiencing isolation and exclusion and coming from rural areas with stronger social cohesion? Similarly, with rural depopulation, can schools provide such an anchor?

INTERNATIONAL DIVIDES OF AFFLUENCE AND POVERTY

Global inequality has increased over the last two hundred years far more than anything experienced in the world before. Global inequality is the result of the spectacular increase in affluence in mainly Western countries in this period. Although some countries (particularly in Asia) are showing fast growth rates, the gap in income between the average citizen in the richest and in the poorest countries is very wide indeed and getting wider. Investment in education and training is increasingly seen as a means of maintaining an edge over a country's economic competitors, raising the issue of how far support for education which is beneficial for the country itself, is also fuelling global inequalities.

Figure 2.3. **The widening gap between richer and poorer world regions**

GDP per capita in international dollars

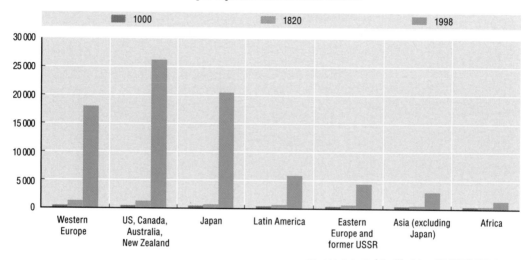

StatLink ᴹˢᴸ http://dx.doi.org/10.1787/403874835183

Source: OECD (2003), *The World Economy: Historical Statistics*.

There is wide inequality between different parts of the world in average personal income (as measured by GDP per person). The advantage enjoyed by the Western world and Japan is very clear in the figure, which also shows how much this has become pronounced in the past 200 years. Whereas in the early 19th century, these different groups of countries were relatively equal and all much poorer than today, by the end of the 20th century the wealthier regions had raced well ahead of the rest of the world.

The next figure shows the evolution of the UN Human Development Index for different regions of the world over the past 30 years. This Index combines indicators for health, education and income, to give a fuller picture than that based purely on economic resources. This fuller index modifies some of the very stark differences, though the OECD countries are clearly and consistently well ahead. The progress of the non-OECD Asian countries is clear and they have managed to close some of the gap with the richest countries. Africa's position is still well behind with little sign of growth in the decade from the mid-1990s.

This international inequality is a key factor running through such problems as environmental degradation, disease transmission and political instability. In a global world, the boundaries around the places which are rich and poor, stable and unstable are not hermetically sealed. What takes place in one region increasingly has ramifications for life in another. For example, more and more people see migration from poverty to affluent societies as the most attractive – or indeed the only – option (see next section).

Education is both a reason for affluence – enhancing the base of knowledge and expertise – and its beneficiary, as prosperity has enabled resources to be available to spend on teachers and facilities far beyond the reach of the poor countries.

Figure 2.4. **Very different levels of human development**

Trends in scores on the Human Development Index (combining health, education and income)

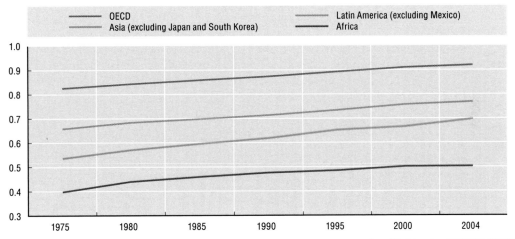

StatLink ═══ http://dx.doi.org/10.1787/403877053018

Source: UNDP (2006), *Human Development Report* (reproduced with permission of Palgrave Macmillan).

And education?

- Whether or not all engaged in improving education do so because it enhances a country's economic competitive edge, this is an important fact with high political resonance. Does national investment in education bringing economic returns inevitably increase global inequalities?

- For the less developed regions, education plays a key role in their economic and social development but how can education be realised under conditions of (extreme) poverty?

- How aware are students in OECD countries about the bigger global problems illustrated by these figures and should they know more about the situation worldwide?

POPULATIONS ON THE MOVE

The movement of populations has been a feature of human life throughout history. This is certainly a feature of today's world with growing immigration to the OECD area as a whole. There is a strong "push" factor from populations looking to escape poverty by moving to one of the world's rich nations, with images of affluence in these countries readily available on TV screens. There is also the "pull" factor from the rich countries, whether by governments looking to revitalise their own ageing societies with "new blood" or by major companies in search of the highly-skilled. Significant levels of migration clearly have profound implications for education in terms of who is in school, family structures and backgrounds, and national cultures. The different forms of migration can have very different implications for education.

Figure 2.5. **More enter than leave OECD countries, with substantial numbers now "foreign-born"**

Percentage of "foreign born" (2004) and net migration (per 1 000 population, 1990-2004)

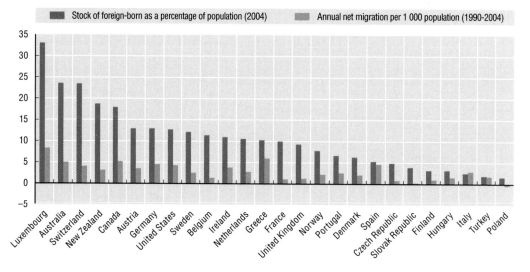

StatLink ▨▨ http://dx.doi.org/10.1787/404022352641

Note: Net migration means the inflow of people minus the outflow of people to a country; a positive net migration means more people are entering then leaving the country.
Source: OECD (2005), *Society at a Glance.*

Averaged across the 1990-2004 period, more now enter than leave all the OECD countries shown (except Poland). OECD countries are now primarily destinations for migrants from other countries. The speed with which change can happen is illustrated by the cases of Spain and Greece: until a generation or two ago such important sources of *emigration* in Europe, they are now clear destinations for *immigration*. This net immigration translates into substantial percentages of "foreign-borns" in many countries which stand at 10% or over in more than half of the countries included above. The largest shares are in Luxembourg (33%), Australia (24%), Switzerland (24%) and New Zealand (19%). That is in sharp contrast to the Slovak Republic, Finland, Hungary, Italy, Turkey and Poland where the share of foreign born was below 5%.

Immigration is a complex phenomenon, with different people migrating for different reasons. The following figure gives a sense of this diversity. The numbers born outside national borders coming from countries with annual average incomes below the

USD 10 700 cut-off have been growing since the mid-1990s in all cases (for the countries with the information). In all the cases, these rates are higher than for "foreign-born" people from countries above this income threshold, although there are wide differences between countries.

Immigrants from the poorer countries are by no means all low-skill or poorly-educated (though many are). The "brain drain" from those countries well below the income threshold, including those who move to become teachers, can have profound consequences on the human capital left in the country of origin.

Figure 2.6. **New foreign-born in OECD countries mainly not from "high-income" countries**

Change in numbers of foreign-born between 1995 and 2004 *from top 15 countries of origin* divided into figures for "high-income" countries and others: per 1 000 population

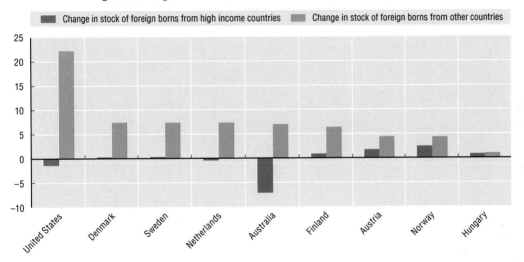

StatLink ⊡⊡⊡ http://dx.doi.org/10.1787/404045188400

Note: World Bank definition of high income: GDP per capita USD 10 726 or more.

Source: OECD (2007), migration datasets.

And education?

- In pluralistic societies, the school comes to face an even greater range of family expectations and aspirations about what it should be doing. How far should different demands be accommodated? What does multi-cultural mean in practice?

- The challenge of combating inequality of educational opportunity grows as newly-migrated families are among those most likely to face precariousness and exclusion. How equipped are schools for this challenge?

- Immigration means that, throughout their lives, pupils will be confronted with culturally diverse environments, whether at school or outside or later. What do they need to learn to deal with this increased cultural diversity?

GLOBAL ENVIRONMENTAL CHALLENGES

From the 1970s onwards there is an increasing awareness that the environment is under threat. Though important policies have been put in place with sometimes visible effects, there remain important challenges, like pollution, deforestation and reducing bio-diversity. The warming of the planet is now an urgent fundamental issue, with an increasing body of evidence that global warming is a result of human activity. The effects will be profound; they include rising sea levels and a reduction in bio-diversity. For education, this is part of the future world that young people will grow up in, and in some locations the impact on educational infrastructure will be very direct. Education plays a key role in shaping the attitudes that can make a difference, while some practices linked to schooling (wasteful car use, for instance) are part of the problem.

Figure 2.7. **Global warming due to human factors**

Global temperature variation without human influence (blue) compared with actual measures (purple)

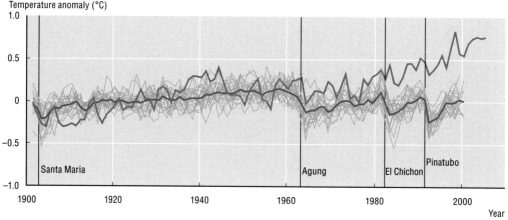

Source: IPCC (2007).

Global temperatures have always fluctuated: they were stable in the 19th century, rose slightly during the first half of the 20th century, fell back until the late 1970s after which they started rising again with now the pace of change quickening. Up to the 1960s changes in the world's climate were to be explained through variations in the angle of the earth's rotation and distance from the sun. Now, the Intergovernmental Panel on Climate Change (IPCC) has established that it is very highly probable (90%) that human activity is responsible for global warming, especially through power generation, deforestation and transport (planes and ships as well as cars). The United States is still the biggest producer of greenhouse gases, but China is closing in and India follows next.

Apart from a direct influence of global warming on rising sea levels and more extreme weather conditions, it also has an impact on bio-diversity. If even the mid-range IPCC's climate change scenario (a 2-3 °C increase by 2100) is correct, forecasts are that between 15% and 37% of the species included in the models would be extinct by 2050. Not all is gloom and doom, however. The next figure shows trends in the emissions of air pollutants, illustrated by sulphuric and nitric oxide levels. Since 1990, there have been major improvements in most countries, with Australia, New Zealand and Turkey among the notable exceptions. This has partly been due to deliberate policy to control pollution, partly through factors such as structural changes in the economy, savings and use of new forms of energy, as well as through technical progress.

On other indicators the situation is mixed. In OECD countries, for example, the areas accounted by forests and woodland have remained stable overall or have even increased slightly. Globally, however, this has been more than counteracted by the continued deforestation in non-OECD, including tropical, countries. Significant progress has also been made in cleaning up industrial and human effluent, especially with the installation of effective water treatment plants. At the same time, erosion and other sources of pollution continue to reduce water quality in some locations.

Figure 2.8. Air pollution going down in most OECD countries

Change (%) in NO_x and SO_x emissions from 1990 to 2002

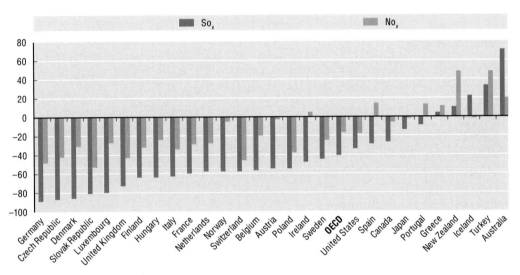

StatLink ᴍ᷿ᔕᴵ http://dx.doi.org/10.1787/404056128100

Note: NO_x and SO_x or Nitrogen Oxides and Sulphur Oxides are polluting gasses.
Source: OECD (2006), *Environment at a Glance.*

And education?

- What roles should education play in shaping the knowledge, attitudes and behaviour which underpin the environmental issues discussed in this section? Are there competing arguments for explicit environmental programmes in the curriculum *versus* the development of critical and civic skills?

- Does and should schooling provide a counterweight to behaviour that endangers the environment? How well do young people develop an awareness of the *future* and the very long-term and combined impact of the many decisions we make in our daily lives today?

- Rising sea levels and extreme weather conditions are related to global warming. This increases risks for certain schools in particular (*e.g.* low lying) areas. How should such risks be addressed, not just by policy but by the teachers and students affected?

FIND OUT MORE

OECD publications used

- OECD (2003), *The World Economy: Historical Statistics*, OECD Publishing, Paris.
- OECD (2005), *Society at a Glance*, 2006 Edition, OECD Publishing, Paris.
- OECD (2005), *Trends in International Migration*, OECD Publishing, Paris.
- OECD (2006), *Environment at a Glance*, 2006 Edition, OECD Publishing, Paris.

Other publications used

- UNDP (2006), *Human Development Report*, UNDP, New York.
- IPCC (2007), "Climate Change 2007: The Physical Science Basis", Chapter 9, Figure 9.5, *www.ipcc.ch*.

Relevant websites

- United Nations, World Population Prospects: The 2006 Revision, online version, *http://esa.un.org/unpp/index.asp?panel=2*, accessed June 2007.
- UNDP Human Development Statistics (2006): *http://hdr.undp.org/en/statistics/*.
- Intergovernmental Panel on Climate Change: *www.ipcc.ch* (accessed June 2007).
- OECD environmental data compendium, 2004 data files: *www.oecd.org/document/58/0,2 340,en_2649_33713_34747770_1_1_1_1,00.html*.

Definitions and measurement

- *Gross Domestic Product (GDP)*: The standard measure of the value of the goods and services produced by a country during a period. *Gross* means that no deduction has been made for the depreciation of machinery, buildings and other capital products used in production. *Domestic* means that it is production by the residents of the country. As many products produced in a country are used to produce other products, GDP is calculated by adding the value added for each product.
- *GDP per capita*: The GDP of a country divided by its total population. GDP per capita is generally used as a proxy for economic living standards, although technically this is not what GDP measures (see definition of GDP).
- *More developed regions*: Comprise all regions of Europe plus Northern America, Australia/ New Zealand and Japan (UN definition).
- *Less developed regions*: Comprise all regions of Africa, Asia (excluding Japan), Latin America and the Caribbean plus Melanesia, Micronesia and Polynesia (UN definition).
- *Least developed regions*: This is a list of 50 countries that satisfy specific criteria (see *www.unohrlls.org/*).
- *High income countries*: Countries with a GDP per capita of USD 10 726 or more (World Bank definition).
- *Urban and rural areas*: *de facto* populations living in areas classified as urban and rural according to the criteria used by each area or country (UN definition).
- *Human Development Index*: Provides a composite measure of three dimensions of human development: living a long and healthy life (measured by life expectancy), being

educated (measured by adult literacy and enrolment at the primary, secondary and tertiary level) and having a decent standard of living (measured by GDP per capita in PPP). The index is not in any sense a comprehensive measure of human development. It does not, for example, include important indicators such as respect for human rights, democracy and inequality. But it provides a more inclusive definition of human development than just GDP per capita.

ISBN 978-92-64-04661-0
Trends Shaping Education
© OECD 2008

Chapter 3

Towards a New Economic Landscape

– THE GLOBAL ECONOMY
– KNOWLEDGE-INTENSIVE SERVICE ECONOMIES

In this section we focus on the ways our economies are developing and transforming, under two broad headings:

- *Globalisation.*

- *Service and knowledge economy.*

Globalisation means that increasingly national economies are linked to each other, forming a global market for investments, goods, services and labour. Competition for these is increasingly international. Many jobs require international travel, co-operation, or contact with providers and customers in other countries. The balance of worldwide economic activities is shifting, with China and India already very major players.

This global economy is increasingly knowledge-intensive. Services are becoming more important in OECD economies, with industry a minority and shrinking source of employment, and the primary sector – agriculture, forestry, mining and fishing – at particularly low levels in most countries. More is being spent on research and development (R&D).

THE GLOBAL ECONOMY

Globalisation means that national economies are at the same time integrating and internationalising. Technological advancement, cheaper transport, and removal of trade restrictions have all contributed to the process. Multinational firms do not limit production to a single country, more firms are becoming global, and those operating in the international arena are more diverse, both in size and origin. The economy is globalising in a different sense as well. Where once economic activity and wealth were concentrated in the western world and Japan, new economic powers like China and India are now rising.

Figure 3.1. **Increasing economic globalisation**

Exports of services and outward flows of foreign direct investments by the G7 countries
(billions of USD current prices)

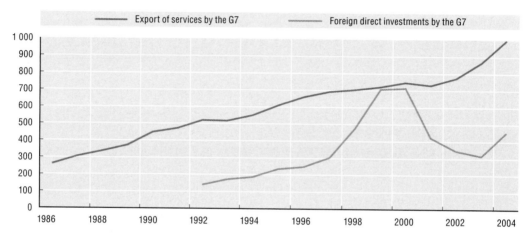

StatLink ⧉ http://dx.doi.org/10.1787/404060482860

Source: OECD (2007), *Globalisation Indicators.*

Foreign direct investment went up spectacularly throughout the nineties and then dipped equally spectacularly after the Internet bubble burst. Since then it has regained importance to be actually three times higher in 2004 than in 1992. Trade in services has been increasing steadily throughout the 1990s and the early years of the 21st century resulting in an almost fourfold increase of trade in services. This development has been continuing at a steady rate, notwithstanding the intervening Internet bubble.

What the figure illustrates is the rise of a global market where capital can be transferred in real time across national borders. Foreign direct investments are especially important because they create long-term links between economies that encourage the transfer of technology and know-how. Apart from services, goods and even labour are increasingly traded on global markets as well. The existence of such global markets raises questions about where national governments fit and their ability to influence these international flows.

The following figure illustrates how globalisation is not just about a growing interconnectedness but also about changing balances of economic power; it illustrates that China's and India's gross domestic product (GDP in purchasing power parities) has grown rapidly and has overtaken in the past decades several of the largest economies in the world. This figure gives an impression of the speed with which this has happened. The

34

growing role and influence in the global economy is changing the geo-political landscape. Hundreds of millions of working-age adults will become available for employment in what is evolving into a more integrated world labour market. This enormous workforce – a growing portion of which will be well educated – represents an attractive, competitive source of low-cost labour especially as technological innovation is facilitating the global movement of jobs.

Figure 3.2. **China and India catching up**

Size of GDP (in purchasing power parities) of the world's six largest economies from 1975 to 2005 in billions

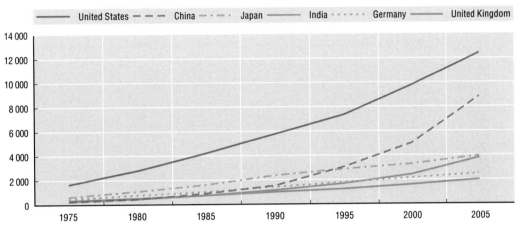

StatLink ⬚⬚⬚ http://dx.doi.org/10.1787/404104023422

Note: In December 2007, a World Bank study led to a 40% downwards revision of China's GDP in PPPs; this would still mean that China is the second largest economy and does not touch the principal of the argument.

Source: United Nations Common Database, online database, *http://unstats.un.org/unsd/cdb/cdb_series_xrxx. asp?series_code=29923*, accessed February 2008.

And education?

- Increasing competition on global markets has underpinned the idea that countries need constant innovation to maintain position. Does education nurture the creativity necessary to be innovative?

- Education and training systems have traditionally been strong bastions of national decision-making. Are they sufficiently sensitive to the international developments described in this section? Are teachers aware?

- Does the growing economic role of Asian countries suggest any change for the curricula and education systems of OECD countries, not just for language teaching but also for other subjects (*e.g.* history, geography)?

KNOWLEDGE-INTENSIVE SERVICE ECONOMIES

While OECD countries have been getting bigger economically, the growth is not evenly spread over all the different kinds of economic activities. Some have grown faster than others and some have tended to decline in importance. The long-term shift to services has continued throughout the final two decades of the 20th century and into the 21st. The shift towards jobs in the service industry often calls for more education. Moreover, the growing knowledge-intensity of the economy calls for very advanced skills and qualifications.

Figure 3.3. **Growth in the service sector**

Sectoral employment shares in 20 OECD countries (excluding those with no data for the full period, most importantly Central and Eastern Europe)

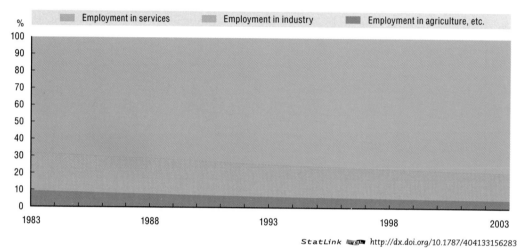

StatLink ⬛🔢 *http://dx.doi.org/10.1787/404133156283*

Source: OECD (2007), STAN database for Industrial Analysis.

The figure shows that services now account for almost all new jobs while in many OECD countries jobs are disappearing in the manufacturing and other industries. In the two decades from 1983 onwards, jobs in the agricultural sector had gone down by 4.6% and in the industrial sector by 6.5%, while in the service economy they had gone up by a further 11% in only 20 years.

Many of the services are knowledge intensive. Most OECD countries are now labelled "knowledge economies" meaning that knowledge is now of predominant importance for economic growth and prosperity. As a consequence, education has moved up on the political agendas as it is now seen as critical to economic growth. Much debate has focused on how far education systems are able to respond to the demands of the knowledge economy.

One of the ways to illustrate the increased knowledge intensity of OECD economies is by looking at the Research and Development (R&D intensity, *i.e.* the amount of money spent on R&D as a percentage of GDP). There is variation over the OECD countries, with some countries showing marked increases (Finland, Korea and Austria) while in some countries (*e.g.* the Netherlands, France) the intensity has slightly decreased. From 1995

TRENDS SHAPING EDUCATION – ISBN 978-92-64-04661-0 – © OECD 2008

to 2006, R&D in the OECD area grew on average by 0.19% which, though it may seem a small number, translates into an increase of USD 284 billion (equivalent to the entire GDP of Austria). Another indicator of knowledge intensity is the share of researchers in the total number of employees in a country. For the OECD area as a whole this grew from 5.7 researchers per 1 000 employees in 1991 to 6.9 in 2002.

Figure 3.4. **R&D intensity is growing in most OECD countries**

Total spending on R&D (both public and private) as a percentage of GDP

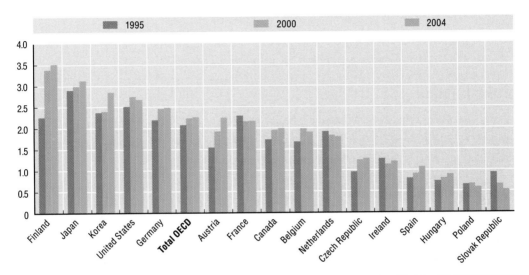

StatLink ⬛ http://dx.doi.org/10.1787/404150678578

Source: OECD (2006), *Science, Technology and Industry Outlook.*

And education?

- Can or should education anticipate the future labour market into which the young people in school today will be entering? Is there a convincing balance of the skills, jobs and trades underpinning vocational education?

- Discussion about the knowledge economy often focuses on the higher education sector and how well it undertakes high-level research and develops research capacity among graduates. But what about schools – are they appropriately equipping the young for the competitive knowledge-based economy and society?

- What does it mean to be in a knowledge-intensive service economy? Should more emphasis be placed on "soft" skills such as caring, judgment, intuition, ethics, inspiration, friendliness, and imagination? How should students develop the capacity to work with others in teams and to innovate, and is this adequately covered?

FIND OUT MORE

OECD publications used

- OECD (2005), *Measuring Globalisation*, OECD Publishing, Paris.
- OECD (2006), *Science, Technology and Industry Outlook*, 2006 Edition, OECD Publishing, Paris.
- OECD (2007), *STAN Database for Industrial Development*, OECD Publishing, Paris.

Relevant websites

- *United Nations Common Database, http://unstats.un.org/unsd/cdb/cdb_help/cdb_quick_start.asp.*
- The Global Transformations website: *www.polity.co.uk/global/.*

Further literature

- Beck, U. (2000), *What is Globalization?*, Polity Press.
- Karoly, L. and C. Panis (2004), *The 21st Century at Work; Forces Shaping the Future Workforce and Workplace in the United States*, RAND Corporation.

Definitions and measurement

- *Foreign Direct Investment (FDI)*: Investments made to acquire lasting interest in enterprises operating outside of the economy of the investor. The *lasting interest* refers to a long-term relationship between the investor and the enterprise and a significant degree of influence on the management of the enterprise (by definition 10% voting power).
- *International trade in services*: International trade in intangible goods. By definition (*IMF Balance of Payments Manual: BPM5*) these include transport, travel, communications services, construction services, insurance and financial services, computer and information services, royalties and licence fees, other business services, cultural and recreational services and government services not included in the list above.
- *Purchasing Power Parities (PPPs)*: PPPs are the rates of currency conversion which eliminate the differences in price levels among countries and make international comparisons possible. For example one dollar in China buys more than one dollar in France, after conversion at the PPP rates into local Chinese and French currencies this dollar will buy the same basket of goods and services in both countries.

ISBN 978-92-64-04661-0
Trends Shaping Education
© OECD 2008

Chapter 4

The Changing World of Work and Jobs

- LIVES LESS DOMINATED BY WORK?
- LESS SECURELY ATTACHED TO THE LABOUR MARKET?
- WOMEN AT WORK

One important aspect of education, alongside others, is preparation for the world of work. It has to do this against the reality that the labour market undergoes important changes. At the same time, what is going on in the world of work and jobs affects the young via the influences of their families and surrounding communities – their prospects, outlook, and personal aims.

We focus on three sets of important issues:

- *Changes in working hours – on an annual and a lifetime basis – to ask whether our lives are now less dominated by work.*

- *Evidence about temporary and part-time employment to ask whether we are less securely attached to the labour market than we used to be.*

- *The continued growing employment of women alongside the gender wage gap.*

LIVES LESS DOMINATED BY WORK?

The trend is for working hours to decrease in Japan, the United States and Europe, with significantly lower working hours in Europe. Careers are also getting shorter, for men at least, while at the same time we live longer and the early years in education are more extended. Female career patterns are moving in the opposite direction. For education, how much time parents have left over from jobs clearly affects the home environment of the student. With such long-term reduction in hours, the life for which schooling is preparation is also a very different one from earlier eras though the place of work in our lives is clearly a more complex matter than just measured time on the job.

Figure 4.1. **People work less**

Annual working hours, 1987-2006 in Japan, the United States and Western Europe

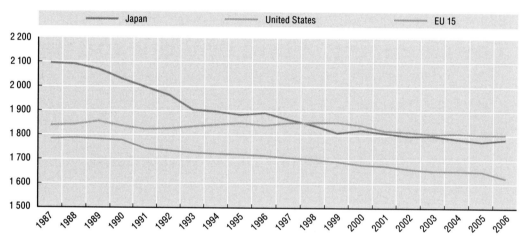

StatLink ⟨⟩ http://dx.doi.org/10.1787/404167531452

Source: OECD (2007), Labour Force Statistics Database.

This figure shows the decrease in the annual working hours per person in certain regions covered by the OECD. The figure refers to all workers, both part-time and full-time so that increasing numbers of part-time workers lower the average even if more part-time workers can mean an increase in the total number of hours worked in the economy. The figure reveals different patterns in different parts of the OECD: significant declines for Japan and Europe, but some increase for the United States over the 1990s coinciding with strong economic growth.

The next figure shows that in most OECD countries, careers – for men – are getting shorter. Older men (50-64 year-olds) stop work earlier now than at the onset of the 1970s, with the biggest changes in the 1970s and 80s (with some reversal of this trend in the 1990s). Retirement and pension options, skill obsolescence, changing job market conditions, and the off-setting employment of partners are all relevant. For women, the situation is very different as the share of older women working continues to rise in almost all OECD countries (except in Poland and Turkey, and [slightly] Greece). The highest labour market participation of older women is found in the Nordic countries and New Zealand.

TRENDS SHAPING EDUCATION – ISBN 978-92-64-04661-0 – © OECD 2008

As work seems to dominate our lives less than it once did – whether looked at from the hours worked per year or the length of the working career being shortened at either end by longer education and earlier retirement – it suggests that greater amounts of time are available for leisure activities. Part of this may be spent on learning activities, whether in formal education programmes or different non-formal arrangements. For those in work, decreased measured hours may well not feel like a reduction due to such factors as long journey times, greater intensity and stress, and blurring boundaries between office life and home life. At the same time, the possibility that a pattern of ever-shortening working years may not be sustainable indefinitely into the future would have direct consequences for education.

Figure 4.2. Careers shorten as fewer – men at least – work beyond age 50

Participation rates of men and women aged 50-64: 1970 and 2004

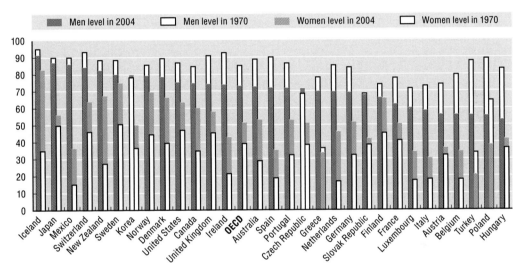

StatLink ⟨≋⟩ http://dx.doi.org/10.1787/404170081568

Source: OECD (2007), Society at a Glance.

And education?

- Increasing leisure time may mean a growing demand for education, especially short-cycle informal learning and "infotainment". Should schools respond to this demand?

- Can young people stay on for ever-longer periods in education, especially if the pattern is for older people in work to stop sooner? Should schools do anything about this or is it a question for tertiary and adult education only?

- Do shorter male working hours get translated into greater availability of fathers to engage in school life? Or do the larger numbers of women working mean that mothers are less available and that parents as a whole actually have less time for school activities?

LESS SECURELY ATTACHED TO THE LABOUR MARKET?

We can examine not only whether people have jobs and how long they work in the year or their lifetime but the kinds of jobs they do. An important dimension to consider is whether there are more or fewer in jobs which offer secure contracts, career opportunities and benefits, including access to training. Two indicators of this are included in this section: the proportion in temporary jobs and the proportion in part-time work. The growth in numbers on temporary contracts, charted over a longer time frame than with part-time work, is more clear-cut: there has been a steady increase in temporary work since the early 1980s. It is therefore important that people leave education with a base of knowledge, skills and qualifications that will give them a firm chance in the job market, including the ability to cope with change and insecurity.

Figure 4.3. **More temporary jobs**

Incidence of temporary work (percentage of total work)

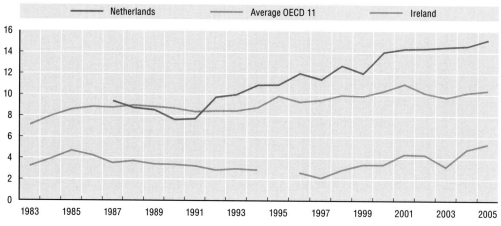

StatLink ᒣᓯᓚ *http://dx.doi.org/10.1787/404185712257*

Note: Selected are those 11 countries for which data are available since the early 1980s (Belgium, Denmark, France, Germany, Greece, Ireland, Italy, Japan, Luxembourg, the Netherlands and the United Kingdom); the average and the countries with the highest and lowest percentages are shown.

Source: OECD, Labour Force Statistics Database.

Evidence for 11 countries offers a 20-year trend in the incidence of temporary work. Not all countries follow the same pathway but the OECD average is clear: there has been a continued increase since 1983 from 6% to 10% of all jobs. In certain countries, the growth has been significantly greater and it now accounts for around 15% of jobs in the Netherlands. This is not sufficient by itself to talk of a "casualisation" of jobs but temporary contracts are now a visible reality of job markets, whether taken from choice or as a last resort.

In looking at attachment to the labour market, there are also the people working "part-time", which in OECD definitions means "less than 30 hours a week". This has traditionally been a source of female employment, leading to the question of whether part-time work is chosen by women as the preferred option or whether it is an illustration of female disadvantage. We can see that many more women continue to work part-time than men: over a quarter of women but less than 10% of working men. There are very modest increases in the proportions in part-time employment for both women and men (on average in the OECD 25.7% in 1994 and 26.4% in 2006 for women; 7.2% and 8.1% for

TRENDS SHAPING EDUCATION – ISBN 978-92-64-04661-0 – © OECD 2008

men). Countries are in very widely differing situations, however. A growing majority of women (60%) are part-time in the Netherlands with sizeable numbers of men, too (16%); in the Slovak Republic with the lowest presence of part-time employees among OECD countries the figures are negligible, and less than 5% even for women.

The trends discussed in this section offer a counterweight to the images of greater leisure presented in the previous section. Temporary and part-time jobs bring their own stresses and demands if job searching continues as a permanent task alongside professional performance, if it means balancing the demanding roles of worker and parent, or if it means rapid change from one workplace to another.

Figure 4.4. **Modest increases in part-time work since 1994**

Percentage of working people in part-time jobs (i.e. less than 30 hours per week) in selected OECD countries (G6 and highest and lowest scoring) by gender

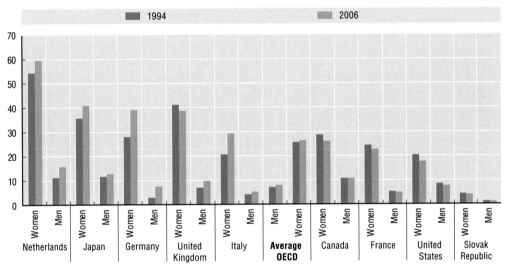

StatLink ▒▒▒▒ *http://dx.doi.org/10.1787/404187382047*

Source: OECD (2007), Labour Force Statistics Database.

And education?

- How well do schools do in preparing young people to cope with, even thrive in, uncertainty? Are the abilities and skills called for in the labour market the same as, or different from, those required in other walks of social and personal life?

- The difficulties of getting a firm foothold in the job market, and of maintaining it, suggest that education systems need to ensure that transition to working life is accepted as a major responsibility. Is this the case or is it common for schools and teachers to treat the economy as a "dirty word" not to sully education's purity?

- How should guidance be offered at the lower- and upper-secondary levels to improve options and opportunities with a view to both educational and professional futures? How well is this done at present?

WOMEN AT WORK

More and more women are now in paid employment. The earlier sections have already described that older women, unlike men, are significantly more likely to be in work than 30 years ago and that a quarter of all working women across the OECD do so on a part-time basis, much higher than do men. But despite this particularity, female participation rates are increasingly catching up with male levels. At the same time, the gender wage gap, while diminishing, stubbornly persists. Education is an integral part of these developments, as both cause and effect. Rising attainment by girls and women is one of most dominant educational trends of past decades; it both results in greater female labour market participation and is stimulated by the changing professional ambitions of women.

Figure 4.5. **More women working**

Percentage of women working in 1994 and in 2005

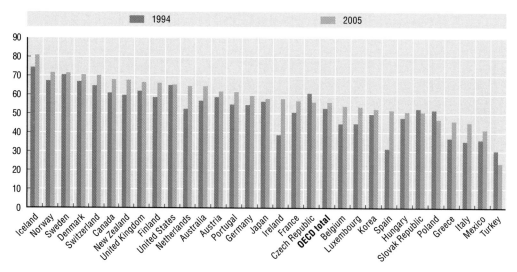

StatLink ⟨⟩ http://dx.doi.org/10.1787/404207228372

Source: OECD (2007), OECD Factbook.

In general, more and more women in all adult age groups once education is completed are now in paid employment. From 1994 until 2005 female employment increased on average by 3% for OECD countries as a whole and in more than half of them it was over 5%. Indeed, in Spain and Ireland this figure reached an astonishing figure of around 20%. The figure also shows that there are exceptions to growing female employment over the most recent period both among countries where it has historically been high like the Czech Republic or low (Turkey). Nevertheless, among the 30 OECD countries female employment has risen in 26 of them since 1994.

The gender wage gap is the compound result of a number of factors: the types of jobs which women tend to do, their greater likelihood to work part-time (although the wage gap is measured by comparing full-time workers, part-time work may have longer-term implications for career prospects), and plain discrimination. Over the past 25 years, the gap has been closing: from an OECD average difference in median incomes of 28% in 1980 the average had fallen to 18% by 2004. Naturally, there are countries above and below the average figures. In one where the gender wage gap is significantly below the overall OECD levels, Sweden, the progress has actually got wider since 1980. What has not been

TRENDS SHAPING EDUCATION – ISBN 978-92-64-04661-0 – © OECD 2008

possible to include in this section, which is also part of the earnings picture, are trends on the particular occupations dominated by either men or women, and the extent to which this segregation has been changing over recent decades.

More women participating in work clearly has a fundamental impact on the living arrangements and home environments of school students. The inexorable rise of female educational achievement and ambition is intricately tied to this phenomenon, as well as being caused by it. Other OECD analysis has shown that the section of the labour market closest to schools – that of teachers – has generally seen rising female participation at all levels; it has resulted in the feminisation of pre-primary and primary schools, in the greater gender balance among secondary school teachers, and in more women becoming school leaders.

Figure 4.6. **Gender wage gap getting smaller but still wide: 1980-2004**

Percentage difference of median incomes of male and female full-time workers
in selected OECD countries

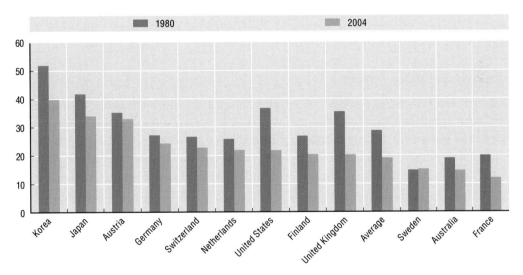

StatLink ⬛⬛⬛ *http://dx.doi.org/10.1787/404216205572*

Note: Countries for which data were available for the full period.
Source: OECD (2006), *Society at a Glance.*

And education?

- What role do schools play, through implicit messages and explicit guidance, in shaping the career and professional (as well as educational) choices of girls and boys? What are the priorities for further change in this respect?

- How are schools experiencing the impact of ever-greater numbers of mothers with full professional careers? Has it changed the balance of responsibilities between schools and families in raising children – for better or worse? – and has it altered relations between fathers and schools?

- How are the trends to greater feminisation of the teaching force being experienced by schools and teachers? Should policy seek to modify the trend and if so in what way?

FIND OUT MORE

OECD publications used

- OECD (2003), *The World Economy: Historical Statistics*, OECD Publishing, Paris.
- OECD (2004), *Employment Outlook 2004*, OECD Publishing, Paris.
- OECD (2006), *Live Longer, Work Longer*, OECD Publishing, Paris.
- OECD (2006), *Society at a Glance*, 2006 Edition, OECD Publishing, Paris.
- OECD (2007), *OECD Factbook 2007*, OECD Publishing, Paris.
- OECD (2007), *Society at a Glance*, 2007 Edition, OECD Publishing, Paris.
- OECD (2007), *Labour Force Statistics Database 1986-2006: 2007 Edition*, OECD Publishing, Paris.

Further literature

- OECD (2001), *The Creative Society of the 21st Century*, OECD Publishing, Paris.
- OECD (2005), *Definition and Selection of Key Competencies: Executive Summary*, OECD Publishing, Paris.

Definitions and measurement

- *Part-time work*: Persons who usually work less than 30 hours per week in their main job. Both employees and the self-employed may be part-time workers. Employment is generally measured through household labour force surveys and, according to the ILO Guidelines, employed persons are defined as those aged 15 or over who report that they have worked in gainful employment for at least one hour in the previous week.

- *Temporary work*: Forms of dependent employment which do not offer workers the prospect of a long-lasting employment relationship: if the work contract specifies that the job lasts a limited amount of time or when a worker is hired to perform a specific and time-limited task. Other cases are less clear-cut and for each country a list of identifiable job types judged to be temporary has been chosen and then used to classify all jobs as either temporary or permanent.

ISBN 978-92-64-04661-0
Trends Shaping Education
© OECD 2008

Chapter 5

The Learning Society

- EDUCATIONAL ATTAINMENT
- RISING INVESTMENTS IN EDUCATION
- GLOBAL EDUCATIONAL PATTERNS – INEQUALITIES AND STUDENT FLOWS

Economies in OECD countries are now often labelled "knowledge economies" and societies also referred to as "knowledge societies". These are broad labels, covering such things as the sheer amount of information available to individuals and firms and ease of accessing it; the rising levels of educational qualifications; and the central importance of knowledge to everyday life and to work.

Learning is clearly pivotal to such information-rich and knowledge-intensive worlds. But we cannot assume that higher levels of educational attainment and investment automatically result in greater learning, nor that they do not bring costs as well as benefits. The issues raised by the major trends and developments regarding education are as complex as in the other fields reviewed in this resource.

In this chapter we identify some of the trends where very major changes and challenges can be identified on the basis of international evidence. (We have avoided statistics referring to the detailed features of educational systems.) The three core areas are:

- *Rising educational attainment.*
- *More resources devoted to education.*
- *Global educational patterns – regional inequalities and international student flows.*

EDUCATIONAL ATTAINMENT

One of the most salient trends in education is the steady increase in attainment. As secondary education has become nearly universalised, the marked expansion of participation in education is better shown by the proportions now reaching higher education. These upward trends – where the dominant international pattern is also for women to have overtaken men – are highly relevant for education, not just as indicative of what is taking place within systems. They mean, for example, that parents as a body have become highly qualified and relate differently to schools. Also, the upward social mobility that becoming a teacher once tended to give has become less important.

Figure 5.1. **Many more people with higher education**

Percentage of population with higher education in age groups 25-34 and 55-64

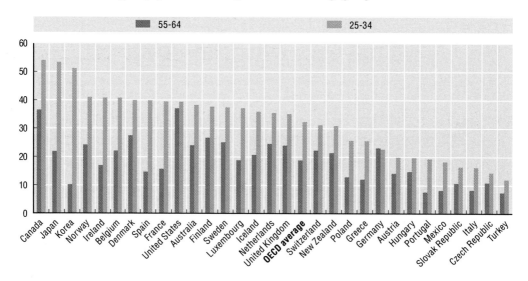

StatLink ⌨ http://dx.doi.org/10.1787/404225215171

Source: OECD (2007), *Education at a Glance: OECD Indicators.*

The last 50 years many OECD countries have witnessed a remarkable expansion of education. The minimum age for leaving education (and training where apprenticeships are part of the compulsory system) has been raised and more and more have stayed on beyond this minimum age. Upper-secondary attainment has become near universal in some countries while higher education has been transformed from an elite experience for the successful few to become mass systems in many countries.

One way to show the scale of the change is to compare the share of younger and older adults with higher education (the broad term covering all "third-level" provision after secondary education). Less than 1 in 5 of those from their mid-fifties to mid-sixties are qualified at the higher level across the OECD as a whole in contrast with the nearly one-third (32%) of 25- to 34-year-olds. The proportion with higher education has gone up by over 20 percentage points between the older and younger adults in Japan, Korea, Ireland, Spain and France (in Korea the increase was more than fivefold from 10% to 51%). In other countries, younger adults are more qualified than the older ones but still less than 1 in 5 holds a higher education qualification (Austria, Hungary, Portugal, Mexico, the Slovak Republic, Italy, the Czech Republic, and Turkey).

The next figure shows that women have slowly but surely overtaken men in terms of both upper secondary and higher education attainments across OECD countries as a whole. Fewer than half of the older 55-64 year-old women are qualified to upper secondary level compared with nearly 60% of the men, but female attainments have risen sharply to approach the 80% mark among younger women thereby overtaking the men where attainment rose by only 17 percentage points. Women's attainment of higher education more than doubled from 16% to 35%, again overtaking men as male attainment only rose by 8% (to 29%).

Figure 5.2. **Women overtaking men for participation in upper secondary and higher education**

Percentage of men and women in upper secondary and higher education for different age groups in the OECD area

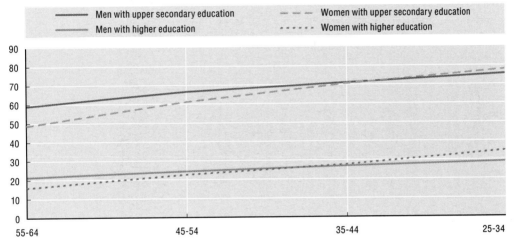

StatLink http://dx.doi.org/10.1787/404228587401

Source: OECD (2007), *Education at a Glance: OECD Indicators.*

And education?

- Do rising levels of educational attainment translate proportionally into higher levels of learning, skills and cultural understanding?

- Are ever-more educated parents proving to be an invaluable educational resource to complement the work of schools? Or are they instead opting out of many schools – moving neighbourhoods or choosing private provision – so depriving schools of their support?

- Levels of educational attainment higher for women than men have become the norm and are historically unprecedented. Why is this happening and will it continue? What will be the long-term social and economic effects?

RISING INVESTMENTS IN EDUCATION

For most OECD countries with the requisite data, spending on education has gone up over the past decade in both absolute terms and per student. These increasing investments have been facilitated by high economic growth in many places, particularly in the second half of the 1990s. Rising investments per school student have also been helped by declining enrolments in some OECD countries. But whether due to the growing priority for education in today's knowledge-intensive world, or to the fortuitous coincidence of smaller cohorts of young people entering schools, the figures reveal a buoyant picture for educational expenditure at least up to the current mid-2000s.

Figure 5.3. **Increasing investments in schooling**

Annual expenditure per student on all education services for primary, secondary and post-secondary non-tertiary education (in equivalent USD, converted using PPPs, on the basis of full-time equivalents)

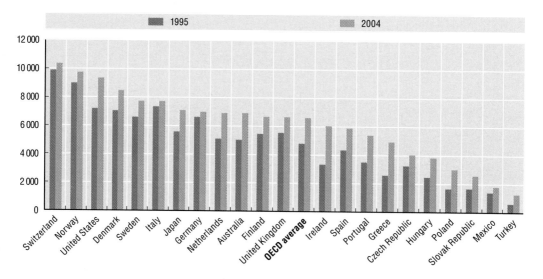

StatLink http://dx.doi.org/10.1787/404238635487

Source: OECD (2007), Education at a Glance: OECD Indicators.

Investments in schooling, expressed as the annual expenditure per school student, have increased from the mid-1990s to 2004 in all the countries for which data are available. Switzerland spends most on its school students, though with only modest spending growth over the past decade. Very sharp increases of 50% or more have taken place in Greece, Hungary, Ireland, Poland, Portugal, the Slovak Republic and Turkey. These sums, expressed in dollars and adjusted to account for inflation, permit direct comparisons over time and across countries.

In most countries, rising expenditure per student is the result of investments in the education system rising faster than the number of students. While some of the growth in resources per learner stems from falling enrolments – it is the main factor in the Czech Republic, Greece, Hungary, Japan, Poland, Portugal and Spain – demographic decline has not been primarily responsible for enhanced "generosity" towards schools elsewhere. As spending is accounted by different items – teacher or principal salaries, administration, buildings and infrastructure, special projects – these overall increases may not always mean greater generosity to those working inside schools.

What makes higher education different from schooling are the rapid increases in student numbers. There have been growing investments in higher education as well, but once this is calculated on a *per student* basis, the investments do not appear so large: they went up from USD 10 145 to USD 11 100 in the OECD area as a whole. In certain countries – the Czech Republic, Hungary, Poland, Portugal, Sweden and the United Kingdom – expenditure on higher education *per student* actually fell between 1995 and 2004, though often by small amounts, mainly because of the rapid growth in student numbers. The figure below is divided into those with rising (left side) and falling (right side) spending per higher education student.

Figure 5.4. **Changing investments in higher education**

Annual expenditure per student on all education services for higher education (in equivalent USD, converted using PPPs, on the basis of full-time equivalents)

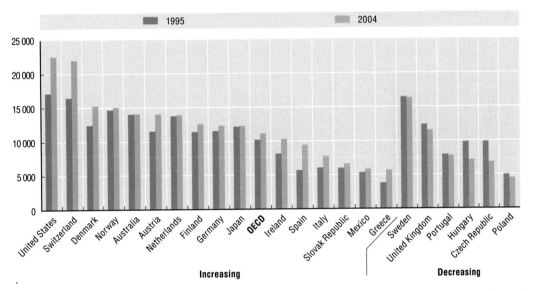

StatLink ⟍ http://dx.doi.org/10.1787/404240745513

Source: OECD (2007), *Education at a Glance: OECD Indicators.*

And education?

- In all OECD countries more money has been available on average per school student. How should that money best be spent? Which investments have the highest rates of return?

- When these spending patterns for schools are combined with those on higher education, it reveals a high public priority for making resources available for education. Is the recent trend likely to continue? What will happen if this dries up?

- High expenditure on schooling does not translate straightforwardly into better results: Finland has around average expenditure but very high achievements while Norway, Italy and the United States spend more for much lower achievements (based on data from the OECD Programme for International Student Assessment, PISA). What can be done to spend money more effectively?

GLOBAL EDUCATIONAL PATTERNS – INEQUALITIES AND STUDENT FLOWS

Trends in two very different aspects of global educational developments are examined in this section. As regards primary education, enrolment levels are going up worldwide but major disparities remain between the rich and poor countries of the world. While the OECD countries have universal primary (and increasingly pre-primary) schooling and are expanding upper secondary and higher education, developing and especially the least developed countries have substantial parts of the population still without access even to primary education. Global inequalities are also reflected in students moving to the OECD countries for higher education, often from the developing regions. The international market for advanced education has expanded four-fold over the past 30 years.

Figure 5.5. **More children in primary education especially in the least developed countries**

Percentage of children of primary-education enrolment age enrolled in primary education

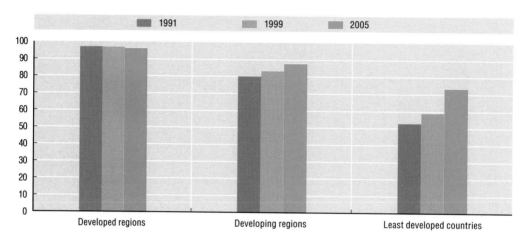

StatLink ⬛️ *http://dx.doi.org/10.1787/404241675133*

Note: There is no established convention for the designation of "developed" and "developing" countries or areas in the United Nations system. In common practice most OECD countries are considered "developed" regions. The definition of least developed countries is clearer: this is a list of 50 countries that satisfy specific criteria (see: *www.unohrlls.org/*).

Source: United Nations Statistics Division.

In almost all countries participation levels in education are rising. In developing regions, participation in primary education has gone up from 80% to 88% and in the least developed countries it has risen even faster from 53% to 74%. But large disparities remain. The UN estimates based on enrolment data show that 72 million children of primary school age were not in school in 2005; of these, 57% were girls. Moreover, the figures are probably overly optimistic, as children may be enrolled but not regularly attend classes. Accurate counts for countries in conflict or post-conflict situations data are also often not available. Hence the global international picture shows that even universal primary education is still not being achieved in many countries.

Looking at the other end of the educational spectrum, a different global trend can be seen in higher education. Over the past three decades, the number of students enrolled outside their country of citizenship in higher education has grown dramatically from just over 600 000 worldwide in 1975 to 2.7 million in 2005 – a more than four-fold increase.

This growth in the internationalisation of higher education has accelerated during the past ten years, mirroring the globalisation of economies and societies.

Looking at the origins and destinations of international students reveals net one-way traffic from the rest of the world towards the OECD countries. In 2005, the large majority of the 2.73 million higher students enrolled outside their country of citizenship were studying within the OECD area (2.3 million or 84%), and of these more than two thirds originated from outside the OECD. Asian students (excluding those from the OECD countries Japan and South Korea) form the largest group of international students studying in the OECD area with 40% of the total and among these, Chinese students are by far the largest group (16.7% of all international students in the OECD area are Chinese). Students from Africa account for 11% and those from South America only 5.7%.

Figure 5.6. **Increasing numbers of international students in higher education**

Number of students in higher education studying outside their country of citizenship worldwide
(in millions)

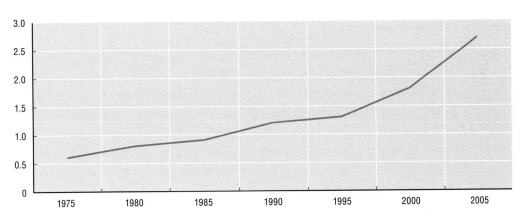

StatLink http://dx.doi.org/10.1787/404338862067

Source: OECD (2007), *Education at a Glance: OECD Indicators.*

And education?

- There is a very positive upward trend in primary education enrolments in the least developed countries as a whole but with major problems and international inequalities remaining. What more might be done, especially by the richer OECD countries?

- More and more students are studying outside their country of residence. Is this a very healthy internationalism breaking down the limits of national boundaries? Or is it richer countries and institutions creating new markets and revenues for their own benefit?

- Is the longstanding notion of "brain drain" still relevant in a globalising world? Is it still taking place with the internationalisation of higher education? Or is internationalisation a way to "fast track" growth in high-level knowledge and skills in countries which cannot rapidly expand higher education themselves?

FIND OUT MORE

OECD publications used

● OECD (2007), *Education at a Glance: OECD Indicators 2007*, OECD Publishing, Paris.

Other publications used

● United Nations (2007), *Millennium Development Goals 2007*, United Nations, New York.

Websites

● UN Millennium Development Goals: *http://unstats.un.org/unsd/mdg/default.aspx.*

Related CERI projects

● **Schooling for Tomorrow:** *www.oecd.org/edu/future/sft.*
● **University Futures:** *www.oecd.org/edu/universityfutures.*

Definitions and measurement

● *Educational attainment:* Attainment profiles are based on the percentage of a certain age group in the population that has completed a specified level of education.

● *Educational levels:* The International Standard Classification of Education (ISCED-97) is used to define the levels of education (for an overview: *www.oecd.org/edu/eag2007,* Annex 3).

● *Expenditure on education per student:* Expenditure on education per student at a particular level of education is calculated by dividing the total expenditure on educational institutions at that level by the corresponding full-time equivalent enrolment. Only those educational institutions and programmes for which both enrolment and expenditure data are available are taken into account.

● *Full-time equivalent (student):* A full-time equivalent (FTE) measure attempts to standardise a student's actual course load instead of assuming that all full-time students study the nominal course load. In countries where there is a significant difference between the actual course load and the nominal one this can lead to different outcomes when calculating for example expenditure on education per student. When actual course load information is not available, a full-time student is considered equal to one FTE.

ISBN 978-92-64-04661-0
Trends Shaping Education
© OECD 2008

Chapter 6

ICT: The Next Generation

- THE DIGITAL REVOLUTION
- THE EXPANDING WORLD WIDE WEB
- TOWARDS WEB 2.0?

Technologies are transforming our world. This is not new. Technological developments like the printing press and the steam engine have had a profound effect on human life. But information and communication technology (ICT) has become a ubiquitous part of our lives in OECD countries. As it is about information and communication, it is of central relevance for education.

The focus is on three interrelated trends:

- *ICT – faster, smaller, cheaper and very widely available.*
- *The rapidly-expanding Internet.*
- *As well as being a source of information, the Internet is being used more actively with users themselves creating the content.*

We focus on ICT while the new transformative technologies in the next decade could well be nanotechnology and biotechnology in combination with ICT – intelligent networks, artificial intelligence and gene manipulation – all with the potential to change human life.

Even taking just ICT, it is clear how profound have been the changes in this domain.

THE DIGITAL REVOLUTION

Information technology has developed very rapidly over the past 40 years, with computers becoming smaller, faster, cheaper, and more powerful. Information technology is now an integral part of our daily lives and embedded in many products. Many of us are now living in technological environments and need to adjust to the rapid pace in which these environments are changing. How easily we can access very large quantities of information very rapidly and in very different settings is clearly a key matter for education.

Figure 6.1. **Computers becoming rapidly faster and more powerful**

Number of transistors on a chip (in millions)

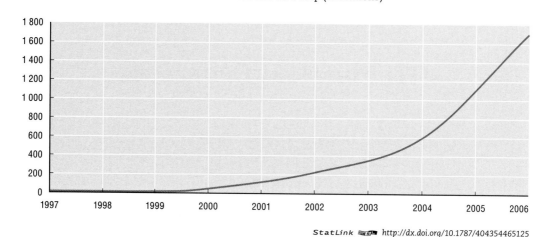

StatLink http://dx.doi.org/10.1787/404354465125

Source: Intel (*http://download.intel.com/museum/Moores_Law/Printed_Materials/Moores_Law_Backgrounder.pdf*) and Wikipedia (*http://en.wikipedia.org/wiki/Transistor_count*).

Computers have become faster very quickly in the last forty years and the hectic pace of change has kept up in the last ten years. The figure shows the number of transistors put on the chip in the central processing unit of the computer – an indication for the speed and power of the computer. Memory disk capacity has been growing exponentially as well. In the meantime the prices to be paid for computing power and memory have been plummeting. Put together, computers have quickly become smaller, more powerful and inexpensive.

In this technological environment, computers have become an integral part of our societies and our lives, transforming such diverse matters as the way we work and relax, how businesses operate, the conduct of scientific research, and the ways governments govern. They are integrating into other technologies – in cars, phones and many other things that used to be "low-tech". There is every reason to suppose that the pace of technological change will continue though we cannot say precisely in which forms and directions.

Despite computers in so many places and domains, there are still large numbers without access to computers even in OECD societies. This becomes a source of exclusion, the more that ICT becomes integrated into daily life for banking, shopping, paying taxes, and the like.

By 2005 (and it will have risen since), access to a home computer had risen to around 80% in Japan and in Germany, Canada and the United Kingdom had reached 70%. We recognise how basic this indicator is. For one thing there are many other forms of technology than the basic home computer. And a pertinent question for education is not "how many households have a PC?" but "how many students have personal access to which devices?"

Figure 6.2. **Towards universal access to a home computer?**

Households with access to a home computer as percentage of total households in G7 countries

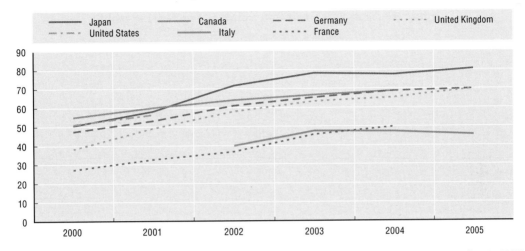

StatLink ⟨≋⟩ http://dx.doi.org/10.1787/404381120822

Source: OECD key ICT indicators: www.oecd.org/sti/ICTindicators.

And education?

- Technological development is taking a very rapid pace. How well have schools kept pace and should they? How can we improve teachers' knowledge and skills and how well adapted is the ICT equipment in schools to learning?

- What are the effects on children of growing up in the digital age? What are the effects on their capacities and needs as learners? In what ways, if at all, should education be organised differently in recognition of the digital environment of young people?

- Does ICT allow for more self-paced, interactive and self-improving styles of learning? How far does, and should, its potential to personalise learning get exploited, whether in schools or in other places where learning can take place?

THE EXPANDING WORLD WIDE WEB

The Internet represents far-reaching and rapid technological development with a multitude of implications for society. By itself the Internet is the system of connected computers, but it has enabled very significant applications like email exchange and the World Wide Web and others like e-banking, on-line shopping, watching TV or making phone calls. Both the physical Internet and the applications available through it have increased rapidly in the past ten years. The challenges for education are much less about student competence or motivation to get involved in the Internet, and more about harnessing its vast potential to enhance learning and about developing critical capacities for its use.

Figure 6.3. **Number of websites worldwide increasing rapidly**

Number of websites in millions

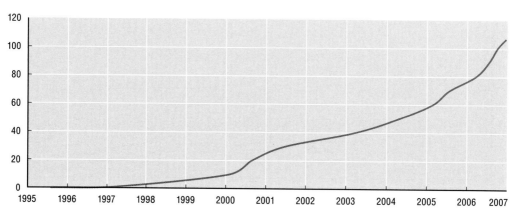

StatLink ⛶ http://dx.doi.org/10.1787/404410374007

Source: Netcraft Surveys, June 2007, *www.netcraft.com/.*

The use of the Internet has exploded in the past ten years, the small number of websites around 18 000 in 1995 mushroomed to over 100 million in 2007. Around 90% of this growth has taken place since 2000. The number of Internet users follows a similar pattern – what must have seemed a large 16 million in the mid-1990s is dwarfed by the over a billion (1 000 million) users by 2006. Broadband access has risen sharply this decade, accounting in Canada for almost 25% of the population by 2006, with an OECD average around 17%.

The Internet is opening up new horizons and possibilities, including educational ones. It offers an enormous and global reservoir of information that can be tapped into for many purposes. It permits cheap rapid international communication (*e.g.* through email) as well as ready access to a wide range of services and products. On the other side are problems such as the information overflow, the valuation of quantity and rapidity over quality, and information pollution (misinformation, pornography, junk e-mail, viruses, etc). Copyright and privacy issues have acquired completely new dimensions.

TRENDS SHAPING EDUCATION – ISBN 978-92-64-04661-0 – © OECD 2008

Equity too is an important area of concern. There is a "digital divide", both within the affluent OECD societies and between richer and poorer countries. Research shows that access to the Internet is positively related to higher levels of income and educational attainment. Men more often have access than women, households with children more than those without, and younger age groups more than older groups. This "universalisation" leaves those still without access even more excluded.

Figure 6.4. **Growing access to broadband Internet connection**

Subscriptions to broadband Internet per 100 inhabitants in G7 countries and OECD average

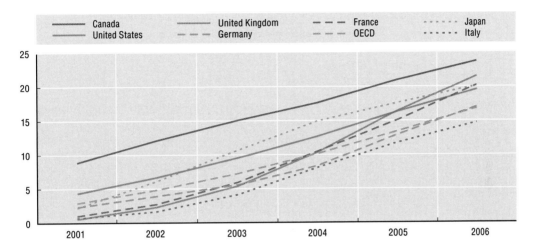

StatLink http://dx.doi.org/10.1787/404416234725

Note: Broadband connections included in OECD data must have download speeds equal to or faster than 256 kbit/s.

Source: OECD broadband portal, *www.oecd.org/sti/ict/broadband*.

And education?

- The progress of ICT is continuously improving the possibilities for networking, distance learning and self-learning. How is this being felt by schools – as an extension of their possibilities or as a threatening alternative?

- With the dramatic increases in the amount of information available, how can schools develop in children the critical capacity to deal with all this information and to separate the important and the trivial, the good and the bad?

- The enormous amounts of information on the Internet can be freely searched using key words and hypertext. How is this affecting the dominant modes of knowledge organisation – for example, undermining knowledge disciplines in favour of more multi-disciplinary, open-ended forms?

TOWARDS WEB 2.0?

The primary use of the Internet has been as a source of information, but now the growing participation and interaction of Internet users is modifying this. The rise of user-created content is becoming a central element of the World Wide Web. Individual Internet users are increasingly making their own personal contributions instead of merely surfing the web. User-created content takes many forms, ranging from sharing short movies (Youtube), pictures (Flickr), to the creation of an on-line encyclopaedia (Wikipedia) or the creation of a personal blog. Though some of this content is doubtless trivial, it signals a development with important parallels in, as well as applications for, education.

Figure 6.5. **Massive growth of Wikipedia**

Number of entries to Wikipedia

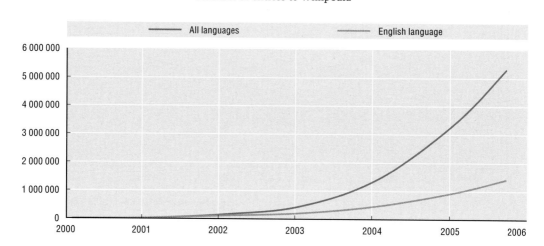

StatLink ⬛🔗 http://dx.doi.org/10.1787/404432623320

Source: Wikipedia, June 2007.

Wikipedia is a project where many authors are together creating an on-line dictionary. It uses technology that allows users to add, remove, and otherwise edit and change content collectively. Users can instantly change the content of the pages or simply format them. Initial authors of articles allow other users to edit "their" content. The fundamental idea behind Wikipedia is that a vast number of users read and edit the articles thereby potentially correcting mistakes. Wikipedia has grown extremely quickly, from scratch at the beginning of 2001 to over 5.4 million articles by September 2006 and is still rising rapidly.

A "blog" is a type of webpage updated at regular intervals which consists of written text, images, audio, or moving images, or a combination of these. Blogs come in many forms for many purposes; some are very personal while others are influential and public. Like Wikipedia, blogs have seen a massive growth – from a few thousand in early 2003 to over 60 million at the end of 2006 (and still growing fast).

TRENDS SHAPING EDUCATION – ISBN 978-92-64-04661-0 – © OECD 2008

These new forms of user creation and distribution are spurring new business models (Amazon, for example, invites people to write reviews on the books they sell). Wikipedia, blogs and the like are presenting challenges to the established media and other industries. Some worry about the lack of quality control and about potentially unreliable sources of information replacing the traditional media, others herald the opportunity precisely to bi-pass traditional channels of information. The established media themselves are part of the change; for example, many newspapers have established on-line editions with blogs attached to them.

Figure 6.6. **Blogs are mushrooming**

Number of blogs tracked by Technorati (in millions)

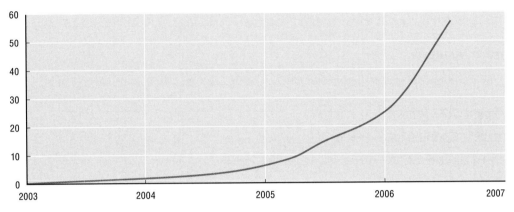

StatLink 🖳🖳 http://dx.doi.org/10.1787/404442801246

Source: Technorati, June 2007.

And education?

- With the availability of so much information it is a frequent contention that teaching factual knowledge in schools is no longer relevant. How important is a factual basis to learning and what should be the approach to teaching the skills to digest and interpret information?

- Educational institutions, teachers, and students are increasingly able to access educational resources on line that are open for any individual or group to use. How important is this form of learning materials and what should be the way ahead?

- With the increase of user-created content, the Internet is no longer just about down-loading – up-loading is becoming important too. Is this undermining the status of schools and established curriculum knowledge or is it reinforcing the quality of education? Or instead is it not especially relevant to the core business of education?

FIND OUT MORE

OECD websites used

- OECD Broadband Portal: *www.oecd.org/sti/ict/broadband*.
- OECD standard technology indicators: *www.oecd.org/sti/ict*.

Other websites used

- Intel (number of transistors on a chip): *http://download.intel.com/museum/Moores_Law/ Printed_Materials/Moores_Law_Backgrounder.pdf*.
- Netcraft (number of websites): *www.netcraft.com*.
- Technorati (number of weblogs): *www.technorati.com/weblog/2006/11/161.html*.
- Wikipedia (number of entries): *http://stats.wikimedia.org/EN/TablesWikipediaZZ.htm*.

Further literature

- OECD (2006), *Information Technology Outlook*, 2006 Edition, OECD Publishing, Paris.

Relevant CERI projects

- **New Millennium Learner**: *www.oecd.org/edu/nml*.
- **Open Educational Resources**: *www.oecd.org/edu/oer*.

Definitions and measurement

- *Broadband*: In OECD terms Internet connection with download speeds equal to or faster than 256 kbit/s.

ISBN 978-92-64-04661-0
Trends Shaping Education
© OECD 2008

Chapter 7

Citizenship and the State

– CHANGING FORMS OF POLITICAL PARTICIPATION
– THE ROLE OF THE WELFARE STATE – SMALLER GOVERNMENT?

The relationship between individuals, the state and society in OECD countries has been undergoing important transformations in the recent decades. For some, the combined effect has been to create a relationship between society and the state that is less hierarchical. For others, it is about leaving more to markets and worrying less about equity. Concerns are expressed from whichever viewpoint that public confidence in the political process has diminished and that there is growing influence exercised by the media.

In this section, we present two sets of trends:

● The changing nature of political participation: from voting to participating but also on women participating in political life.

● The nature of government itself as many countries have attempted to "roll back" the welfare state and shift the balance of responsibilities.

There are many other trends which are relevant to education but for which we do not have international figures. The international dimension is itself relevant for many countries: the extent to which the locus of power and influence has shifted to the supra-national level also changing the conventional mechanisms of national public policy-making (including education).

CHANGING FORMS OF POLITICAL PARTICIPATION

Traditionally, political parties and electoral processes have been the primary means of participating in the political process. The concern is that people are increasingly critical – or apathetic – towards institutionalised authority, with damaging consequences for the political process. And, the evidence suggests that fewer people show up for elections, some notable recent exceptions notwithstanding. But this can be set against a trend for more people to engage in alternative forms of political participation and expressing their preferences directly on specific issues. As for participation in politics, a clear trend is towards the growing representation of women in national parliaments, albeit from very low starting points in many countries. For education, the extent to which civic and social responsibility is fostered through schooling, and how this sits with other goals such as improving cognitive outcomes, are obvious questions.

Figure 7.1. **Voter turnout tending to decline but with alternative participation rising**

Voter turnout and % of respondents that took part in various other forms of political action in selected OECD countries from 1975 to 1999

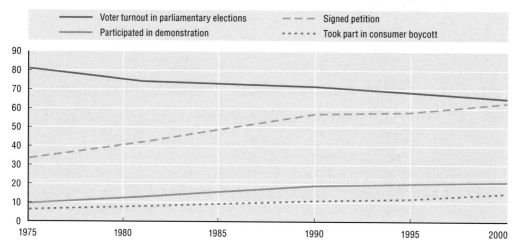

StatLink http://dx.doi.org/10.1787/404456504461

Note: OECD countries included are: Austria, Finland, Germany, Italy, the Netherlands, Switzerland, the United Kingdom and the United States.

Source: IDEA, 2002 (for voter turnout – reproduced by permission of International IDEA © International Institute for Democracy and Electoral Assistance 2008) and World and European Value Surveys (for alternative forms of political participation).

Voting figures for eight countries suggest a decline of interest since the 1970s. Many countries are facing diminishing levels of conventional political participation as well as declining party membership. The general trend to lower voter turnout can be bucked, however, as happened in the recent French and Dutch elections. Alongside signs of wavering conventional political participation, engagement in other forms of political action seems to be on the rise, such as signing petitions, participating in demonstrations and engaging in boycotts. Other OECD analysis has identified a rise in specific-issue engagement. The mushrooming of Internet activity, described above, may well be playing its part in this.

Though one form of activity appears to be replaced by another, it is a matter for concern if interest and engagement in elected parliaments and governments continue to

TRENDS SHAPING EDUCATION – ISBN 978-92-64-04661-0 – © OECD 2008

decline. On the positive side, direct participation may suggest more informed decision-making and the empowerment of citizens and local communities.

Not just voter behaviour but those being voted for have changed. The figure below provides two clear messages as well as showing how different are the national cultures regarding the position of women in politics. First, men still dominate the parliaments of OECD countries: on average with a ratio of 3 to 1. In some countries, the domination is far greater, and in particular cases (Hungary), is even getting worse. The second, more positive message is that the female share of parliamentarians is growing almost everywhere and at a rapid rate from a low starting point. The average gain has been from 15% to 25% in only 15 years, and in some (such as Belgium, Austria and Australia) the increase has been dramatic. The Nordic countries are clearly well out in front.

Figure 7.2. **More women in parliaments**

Share of women in parliaments in selected OECD countries

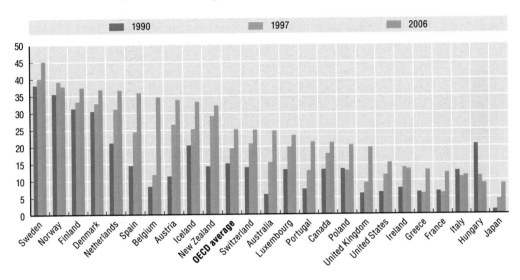

StatLink 🖳 http://dx.doi.org/10.1787/404512666002

Note: Countries for which data for all three periods are available.

Source: OECD (2007), *Women and Men in OECD Countries.*

And education?

- Developing responsible, active citizenship is fundamental to any system of education. What should be the specific role of schools in fostering civic literacy? Does this compete with other goals about conventional outcomes for school time and priority?

- Should schools help build the attitudes necessary for fruitful participation by giving pupils more opportunities to be heard, to participate and to collaborate in school decision-making?

- How, if at all, might the greater voice of women in politics impact on education?

THE ROLE OF THE WELFARE STATE – SMALLER GOVERNMENT?

In the aftermath of World War II, consensus emerged in many countries on the need for active government and publicly-organised services to assure the core business of social protection, health, old age pensions, and education. From the 1980s onwards, there has been a shift – more visible in some countries than others – towards making governments smaller, decentralised, with a greater role for market-type incentives. Where it has happened, it has been inspired by different motives, whether to reduce expenditure, to recognise the marked improvements in affluence after the immediate post-world-war period, to enhance efficiency, to be more responsive to consumer demand, or simply on ideological grounds. Countries are in very different positions regarding the importance of public expenditure and the size of the public sector workforce, both of which have direct consequences for school education. In general, there has not been a radical reduction in public government.

Figure 7.3. **Modest falls in the government workforce**

Government workforce as percentage of total workforce in selected OECD countries

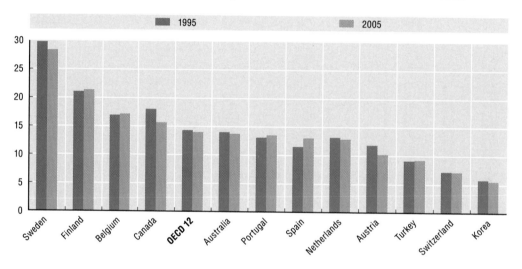

StatLink ⟨⟩ http://dx.doi.org/10.1787/404545042844

Note: 1995, 2005 or nearest available year.

Source: OECD (2008), "Employment in Government in the Perspective of the Production Costs of Goods and Services in the Public Domain" (*www.oecd.org/LongAbstract/0,3425,es_2825_495698_40027479_1_1_1_1,00.html*).

The public government workforce shows wide differences between countries, from around 5% in Korea to almost 30% in Sweden. There have been modest declines in the proportional numbers of government workers, from an average 14.2% in 1995 to 13.9% in 2005 but this is the result of some countries reducing while other countries increasing the percentage of government workers as a percentage of total workers. Canada's over 2 percentage point drop stands out. All this suggests that behind a new discourse has been a less clear-cut underlying reality. Even when decentralisation or privatisation has taken place, this has often been accompanied by dense regulations – suggesting that changing responsibility does not necessarily mean smaller government.

From the 1980s, public expenditure grew steadily as a proportion of a growing economic base albeit less quickly than it had in the 1960s and 1970s. The OECD average peaked at around a fifth of GDP (20.4%) in 1993. Since then, it had fallen back by around one percentage point by 2000 when it started to rise again until 2003 to a level above the 1993 peak level. Alongside, private social spending in OECD countries has on average increased slowly but steadily since the 1980s to stand now at around 3.2% of GDP. Behind the averages are substantial country differences.

Behind this indicator lies a wide diversity of programmes which share the aim of shifting social responsibilities from the state to individuals and companies, with policies aimed at, for instance: re-integrating the unemployed in the workforce; making companies responsible for part of the social welfare of their employees; privatising insurance systems in healthcare; introducing or raising tuition fees in higher education, etc.

Figure 7.4. **Gradually increasing public and private social spending between 1980 and 2003**

Gross public social spending and private social spending as % of GDP in the OECD area from 1980 to 2003

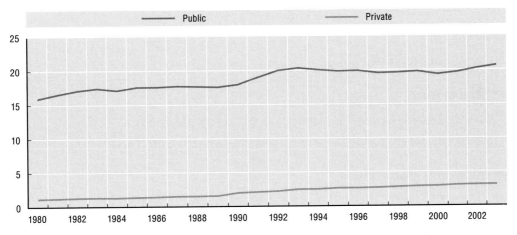

StatLink ⬛🖳 http://dx.doi.org/10.1787/404555237303

Note: Social spending by OECD definition includes: cash benefits (*e.g.* pensions, income support during maternity leave, and social assistance payments), social services (*e.g.* childcare, care for the elderly and disabled) and tax breaks with a social purpose (*e.g.* tax expenditure towards families with children, or favourable tax treatment of contributions to private health plans).

Source: OECD Social Expenditure Database.

And education?

- If individuals are expected to make decisions about healthcare, pensions, higher education financing, etc., which used to be the responsibility of the state, what kinds of knowledge and skills do they need to function in this environment? Do schools need to do more in this regard?

- Where greater reliance is being made on private spending on education, what will be the consequences for the equity of the schooling system?

- If there is generally more of a shift in discourse than actual change, is this a good or bad thing with regards to education?

FIND OUT MORE

OECD publications used

- OECD (2006), Draft report from the project "Management in Government: Comparative Country Data".
- OECD (2007), *Women and Men in OECD Countries*, OECD Publishing, Paris.
- OECD Social Expenditure Database: *www.oecd.org/els/social/expenditure*.

Other publications used

- IDEA (2002), *Voter Turnout since 1945: A Global Report*, International IDEA, Stockholm.
- Inglehart, R. and C. Catterberg (2002), "Trends in Political Action: The Developmental Trend and the Post-Honeymoon Decline", *International Journal of Comparative Sociology*, Vol. (43), pp. 300-316.

Websites used

- IDEA website: *www.idea.int*.

Further literature

- OECD (2002), *Governance in the 21st Century*, OECD Publishing, Paris.
- OECD (2006), *Society at a Glance*, 2006 Edition, OECD Publishing, Paris.

Definitions and measurement

- *Social expenditure*: To be considered *social*, benefits have to address one or more social goals. Benefits (whether cash benefits, direct *in-kind* provision of goods and services, or tax breaks with social purposes.) may be targeted at low-income households, but they may also be for the elderly, disabled, sick, unemployed, or young persons.

ISBN 978-92-64-04661-0
Trends Shaping Education
© OECD 2008

Chapter 8

Social Connections and Values

- LIVING IN MORE DIVERSE FAMILIES
- LESS SOCIAL INTERACTION?
- EVOLVING VALUES

This section focuses on the connections between individuals and their social and cultural environments, affecting the ways in which people live. Firm evidence is not widely available on many of the cultural and social factors relevant to education. This section focuses on three areas where international data permit through-time comparisons:

- Diversifying family arrangements.
- Community and social connections.
- Changing values.

It is often difficult to be objective about developments regarding the family as a social unit; it is a charged emotional subject. Our purpose in describing trends in marriage, divorce and single-parenthood is not to propose any moral agenda but to outline some of the facts of family diversification with undoubted significance for education.

The nature of the "glue" which holds society together is sometimes called "social capital". It refers to the richness of the connections between people and the extent to which they share norms of trust and co-operation. It is common now to maintain that social capital is declining as we live more individualistic, unconnected lives with falling levels of trust. The evidence suggests that, internationally, the situation is not that clear-cut.

Values are notoriously hard to capture using "hard" measurement. The World Values Survey has been conducted for many years and in many countries to give a unique international source on subjective trends. The value trends show continuing wide differences among countries alongside some shared broad tendencies.

LIVING IN MORE DIVERSE FAMILIES

The concept of family is not an unchangeable one. In the 19th century, extended families were important economic units as well as social networks. The nuclear family, where the mother took care of the children and the father worked outside the home was particularly strong in the first half of the 20th century. Family structures continue to change: marriage is less prevalent; couples are increasingly living together without being married; separations and divorces are common; and one-parent families are increasing. The nuclear family is fragmenting towards more complex configurations of home life, at the same time as migration increases the diversity of family patterns. These obviously impact on education, given the centrality of home-school relations to educational success.

Figure 8.1. **Fewer married couples**

Annual number of marriages (left) and divorces (right) per thousand population

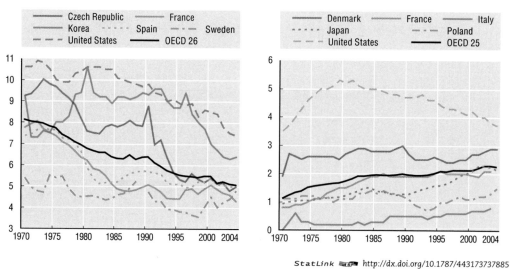

StatLink ⬛🔗 http://dx.doi.org/10.1787/443173737885

Source: OECD (2006), *Society at a Glance*.

Marriage rates have fallen in almost all OECD countries over the period 1970 to 2004 – from over 8 marriages per 1 000 population each year across the OECD as a whole to only 5. The figure shows how different the positions and pathways have been with certain countries showing some increase in the popularity of marriage in the 1970s before falling in the 1980s or, as in Korea, more recently than that. Other countries are consistently below the line with fewer and falling marriages throughout the past 35 years. The divorce rate has followed a complementary upward path and was twice the level of 1970 for the OECD countries as a whole by 2004. There are wide variations, particularly with certain countries (Italy, for example) with divorce still well down on the majority, albeit rising. The United States has seen a drop from the very high levels of the 1970s but maintains its position well above the rest. Other OECD figures show that the percentage of marriages ending in divorce had reached approximately a third in much of West and North Europe and a half or more in the United Kingdom and the United States.

Related to this is lone-parenting. As many as a fifth to a quarter of households with children are now headed by a single parent. The trend in all countries is upwards, though with some very wide differences, such as between the 8% and 28% in Japan and New Zealand respectively.

This means that children grow up in increasingly complex and varied living arrangements. The nuclear family is still prominent but increasingly children live in single parent families, in "reconstructed" families where one or both parents have found a new partner (possibly with their own children), or are physically moving between parents. The chances increase of children moving in and out of these situations. As part of this are the rapidly-falling births – fewer children – outlined above. The growing socio-cultural diversity, on the other hand, means that certain sections of society maintain more traditional family patterns. The diversity which increasingly characterises family life is mirrored in a wide range of emotional and economic situations in which young people find themselves.

Figure 8.2. **More single-parent families**

Percentage of households with one parent

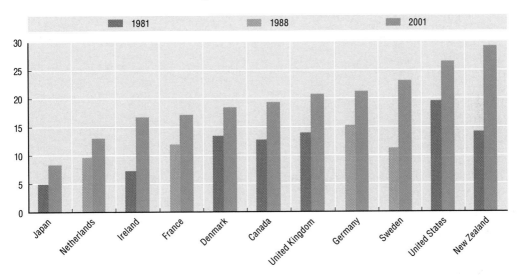

StatLink ▦▦ http://dx.doi.org/10.1787/404580122178

Note: Starting points are 1981, 1988 or the closest available year; end points are all 2001 or closest available year.

Source: The Clearing House on International Developments in Child, Youth and Family Policies at Columbia University, except New Zealand from the 1981 and 2001 Population Census.

And education?

- Effective education relies on good home-school relations. Does the growing diversity of family situations affect the nature of these relations?

- Is the predominance of women teachers, especially at pre-school and primary level, combined with growing single-parenthood creating a long-term imbalance with many children having no male role models?

- Does the diversification of family forms mean a changing balance of responsibilities between the school and the home? Can schools and teachers take on more responsibility for socialising children and should they?

LESS SOCIAL INTERACTION?

What sort of society and community do we live in? Everyday experience tells us that there is more mobility and fewer stable residential and social communities. Material affluence (next section) is part of the picture as the needs of individual families are less tied to their immediate neighbours. We seem to live in a more individualistic world, with a declining sense of belonging to the traditional reference points of community, church or workplace. At the same time, the notion of a "network society" would suggest that belonging is changing not disappearing. What does the evidence show about engagement in social activities, clubs, and societies? Is there more or less trust and co-operation than before? These are important questions for education and particularly for schools. If people are more individualistic, this will promote consumer behaviour in education at the expense of social goals; if social ties are decreasing, this places still more pressure on schools to provide a source of connection.

Figure 8.3. **No general decline in membership of voluntary organisations**

Percentage of people involved in at least one voluntary association

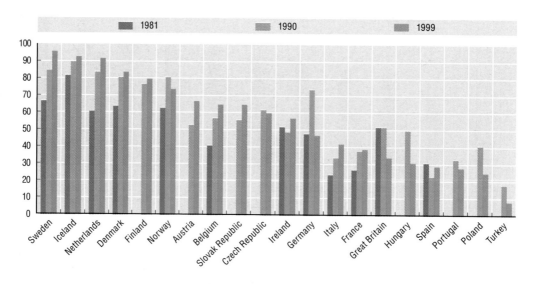

StatLink ⬛⬛ *http://dx.doi.org/10.1787/404645241170*

Note: Based on self-reporting.

Source: World Values Surveys, 1980, 1990; European Values Survey, 1999.

The evidence of the final two decades of the 20th century does not confirm any general pattern of declining social activity, as indicated by membership of voluntary organisations. This is despite decreasing involvement in traditional organisations like churches and trade unions. Membership of voluntary organisations is high and growing in the Nordic region and certain other European countries, is stable or fluctuating elsewhere, but seems to be falling in the United Kingdom, some Central Eastern European countries, Portugal and Turkey. The same country pattern emerges for an indicator of more deliberate engagement – undertaking unpaid voluntary work. The key finding over and above wide national differences is that engagement appears to be growing in places where it is high and declining in some of the places where it is low; in other words the differences in social activity between countries are getting wider.

Asking instead the question, "Do you in general trust other people?" (to be answered "yes" or "you can't be careful enough") reveals again in the Nordic countries and the Netherlands that generalised trust is high, even rising, while in several Southern and Central Eastern European countries it is lower and falling. This is a very general question, of course, and it does not reveal situations in which people have high or low trust. Nor does it shed light on whether particular categories of people (*e.g.* politicians, civil servants, and teachers) are more or less trusted.

Low levels of organisation membership broadly go hand-in-hand with low levels of trust. It is not a perfect fit: Portugal and Spain have both low scores on voluntary organisation membership, but while trust is lower in Portugal than in any other country shown, Spain comes right after the high trust Nordic countries. These data do suggest that the quality of social relations needs attention and is declining in some countries.

Figure 8.4. **Trusting others – wide variation, no clear trends**

Percentage of World and European Values Survey respondents saying that "in general they trust people"

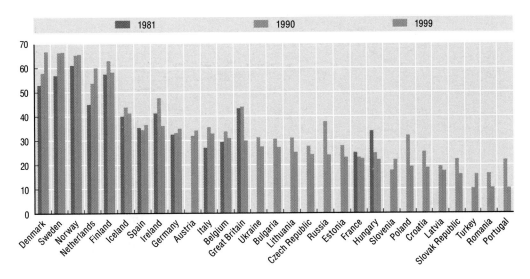

StatLink http://dx.doi.org/10.1787/404653204216

Source: World Values Surveys, 1980, 1990; European Values Survey, 1999.

And education?

- If trust and social engagement are low, in a country or region, where does this leave schools?

- Is the quality of social relations one of the ingredients of educational success? To what extent does learning depend on trust?

- If membership of voluntary organisations is low because of busy professional lives squeezing out available time, are schools finding parents similarly unavailable?

EVOLVING VALUES

Values are core to society but by their nature difficult to grasp through measurement. The World Values Survey has been tackling this challenge for many years and this section reports some main findings. The general trends pattern is that each age band, people born in successive decades, place greater emphasis on self-expression and quality of life, and less emphasis on the traditional sources of authority (religion, family, and nation). Although these are worldwide developments, large differences between different groups of countries endure. Education is essentially about values and the school is one of the places where each generation comes to acquire the values of society. If values change in the broader society, this will have a strong if diffuse impact on what goes on in schools.

Figure 8.5. **Global value change – more secular, more oriented to self-expression**

Factor analysis of value positions of different generations in different regions

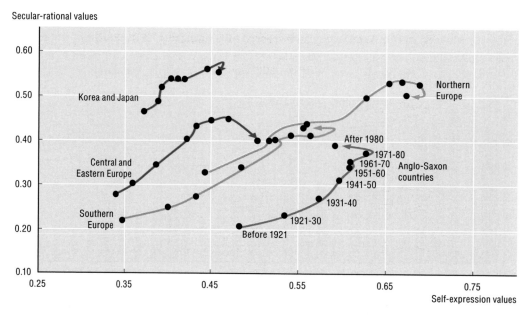

StatLink ᵃᵖ http://dx.doi.org/10.1787/404674051553

Note: The figure is the result of a factor analysis in which a number of variables co-varying are taken to stand for an underlying factor, in this case Secular Rational Values and Self-Expression Values.

Source: World Values Survey, adapted from presentation by Welzel (*www.worldvaluessurvey.org*).

The World Values Survey has found distinct and global trends in expressed values: the generations born more recently express stronger values towards the secular-rational and self-expression values than those born longer ago, but with clear differences between groups of countries. The most recent ten-year age band born after 1980 do not always follow the trend, but this may be more an expression of youth than indicative of any permanent bucking of the long-term trend. Stronger secular-rational values are associated with the decline in religious engagement, and other orientations are closely linked to it: less deference to authority; greater tolerance to divorce, abortion, euthanasia, and suicide; and lower nationalism. Stronger self-expression means lower emphasis on economic and physical security and more on subjective well-being and quality of life. Other related orientations are: lower stress on diligence and hard work, and more on imagination and tolerance as important values to teach.

The value orientations found in different parts of the world remain intact, despite shared rising affluence and a range of shared global influences. The Northern European and Far East countries share the highest secular-rational orientations, but with clearly greater valuation of self-expression among the Europeans. The North European and Anglo-Saxon countries have the greatest orientation to self-expression but with distinctly lower secular-rational values for the Anglo-Saxon countries.

Wishing for "greater respect for authority" can be indicative of a traditional outlook or it may indicate uncertainty in the face of rapid change. The sets of countries with the lowest felt need for more authority are those with the highest secular-rational scores in the first figure – Nordic countries and particularly Korea and Japan. There is very wide variation in the desire for more respect for authority – from 70% in the United States to less than 5% in Japan. Interesting are the several countries where the survey suggests a decline in desire for authority in the 1990s followed by an upturn by 2000.

Figure 8.6. **Wanting greater respect for authority: 1981-2000**

Respondents answering "yes" when asked whether greater respect for authority is a good thing in selected OECD countries

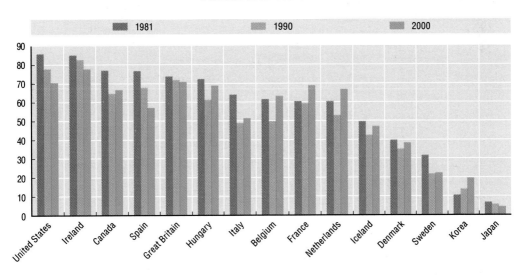

StatLink ⧉ http://dx.doi.org/10.1787/404704152621

Note: Data selected are for the countries for which information is available in the World Values Survey.
Source: World Values Survey.

And education?

- If younger generations of pupils *and* teachers find authority less important, what are the consequences for social dynamics in the classroom and more fundamentally for the role of teachers and the authority of school knowledge?

- If self-expression is generally more valued, should schools do more to develop the ability of self-expression? Or instead should they focus on the social objectives which may not be effectively fostered elsewhere?

- Global diversity of values appears to be an enduring phenomenon. In a globalising world this will mean that students will need the ability to deal with people with different values. What should schools do to contribute to value sensitivity?

FIND OUT MORE

OECD publications used

● OECD (2006), *Society at a Glance*, 2006 Edition, OECD Publishing, Paris.

Other publications used

● Welzel, C. (2006), "A Human Development View on Value Change Trends (1981–2006)", presentation available on: *www.worldvaluessurvey.org*.

Websites

● World Values Survey: *www.worldvaluessurvey.org*.

● The Clearing House on International Developments in Child, Youth and Family Policies at Columbia University: *www.childpolicyintl.org/*.

Further literature

● Inglehart, R. and C. Welzel (2005), *Modernization, Cultural Change and Democracy*, Cambridge University Press.

● Inglehart, R. and W. Baker (2000), "Modernization, Cultural Change and the Persistence of Traditional Values", *American Sociological Review*, Vol. 65.

● Inglehart, R. (2000), "Globalization and Post-Modern Values", *The Washington Quarterly*, Winter, pp. 215-228.

● OECD (2001), *Well-being of Nations*, OECD Publishing, Paris.

● OECD (2001), *What Schools for the Future?*, OECD Publishing, Paris.

● Putnam, R.D. (2000), *Bowling Alone: The Collapse and Revival of American Community*, Simon and Schuster, New York.

Definitions and measurement

● *Single parent families*: Families where single parents live with their dependent children. Dependent children are all children under age 16 and economically inactive youngsters of 16 to 24 who are living in a household with at least one of their parents. Cohabiting couples, another growing family type, are no longer counted as single parents, at least in most countries.

● *Membership in voluntary organisations*: The data here are based on the World Values Surveys of 1981, 1990 and 1999. The survey contains a list of voluntary organisations like charities, religious organisations, education and arts groups, human rights groups, sports groups (with some alterations over time) and then asks: "Which, if any, do you belong to?"

● *Traditional/Secular-rational and Survival/Self-expression values*: These two dimensions explain more than 70% of the cross-national variance in a factor analysis of ten indicators – and each of these dimensions is strongly correlated with other important orientations (World Values Survey).

● *Traditional/Secular-rational values dimension*: Reflects the contrast between societies in which religion is very important and those in which it is not. A wide range of other orientations are closely linked with this dimension. Societies near the traditional pole emphasise the importance of parent-child ties and deference to authority, along with absolute standards and traditional family values, and reject divorce, abortion, euthanasia, and suicide. These societies have high levels of national pride, and a nationalistic outlook. Societies with secular-rational values have the opposite preferences on all of these topics.

- *Survival/Self-expression values dimension*: Reflects the extent to which priorities have shifted from an overwhelming emphasis on economic and physical security towards an increasing emphasis on subjective well-being, self-expression and quality of life. Self-expression values give high priority to environmental protection, tolerance of diversity and rising demands for participation in decision-making in economic and political life.

ISBN 978-92-64-04661-0
Trends Shaping Education
© OECD 2008

Chapter 9

Sustainable Affluence?

– GROWING AFFLUENCE, GROWING ENERGY CONSUMPTION
– INEQUALITY ON THE RISE
– LIFESTYLES WITH HEALTH RISKS

Almost all OECD countries have witnessed growing affluence in the 20th century, especially since World War II. Better material conditions bring many positive consequences but they bring others, too.

Growing energy consumption, for example, with the associated problems of depleting limited energy sources and pollution. Also, though overall prosperity has risen, some have benefited much more than others. High consumption and different lifestyles have brought new health risks, including obesity.

These questions are covered in this section:

- Growing wealth and growing energy consumption.

- Inequality and persistent poverty.

- Lifestyle-related health risks.

GROWING AFFLUENCE, GROWING ENERGY CONSUMPTION

Economic growth across OECD countries has meant improving living conditions for most of their citizens. Many developing countries especially in Asia and to a lesser extent in South America have witnessed improved living conditions, albeit with very large differences between and within countries. With affluence comes greater consumption, so raising issues of how sustainable are our current collective habits – how much we consume and our lifestyles. And with affluence comes resources to pay for education but also a possible tendency to treat education as a private rather than a public good.

Figure 9.1. **Growing affluence**

GDP per person in groups of OECD countries 1970-2005 (in USD, current prices and PPPs)

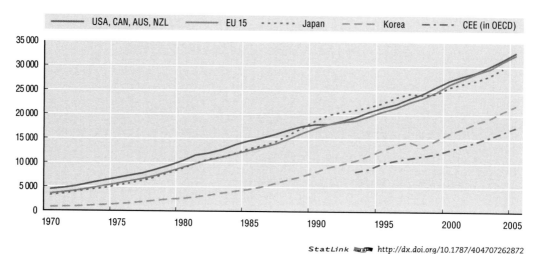

StatLink ⬛⬛⬛ http://dx.doi.org/10.1787/404707262872

Source: OECD (2007), OECD Factbook.

There is growing wealth across the already-rich countries of the OECD (expressed as GDP per capita). The United States, Canada, Australia and New Zealand, European Union countries (EU 15) and Japan show very parallel pathways of growing prosperity over the past 35 years. Korea is now catching up very rapidly in relative terms (in 1970, the EU 15 were 4.5 times richer than Korea, reduced to only 1.5 by 2005). The former Communist OECD countries (CEE: Hungary, Poland, the Czech and Slovak Republics) have more than doubled their prosperity in the past decade.

Increasing levels of wealth have had important impacts on habits, values and attitudes. Some refer to "post-materialism", meaning that as people are liberated from the most immediate stresses of materialistic needs, they come to focus more on personal development and freedom. The earlier section on social change has confirmed the greater emphasis that people are giving to the values of self-expression.

The enormous increase in energy use witnessed over the past three decades or more is shown below. As opposed to a worldwide production of only 5 500 TWh in 1971, this had more than tripled to 17 450 TWh by 2004; current projections by the International Energy Agency are that this will almost double by 2030 to 33 750 TWh. With prosperity has come a seemingly insatiable thirst for more, which raises sustainability issues in a world of limited resources and growing populations. One form of solution without dramatically curbing energy use is the switch to renewable sources. Hydroelectricity generation grew in absolute terms but fell as the share of the total from 23% in 1971 to 16% in 2004, and other alternative sources of electricity are still only marginal (although tripling from 0.7 to 2.1%). Coal, which is the most polluting source of generation, is still the most common and has maintained an almost constant 40% of the total throughout the 1971 to 2004 period.

Figure 9.2. Growing energy (electricity) consumption, coal generation still most common

World electricity generation by source of fuel in Terawatt hours (TWh)

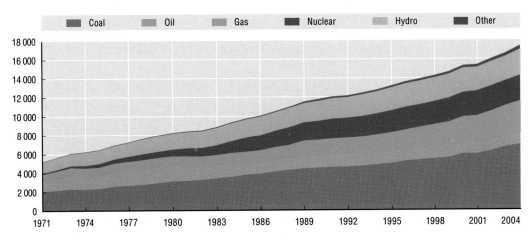

StatLink ⬛ http://dx.doi.org/10.1787/404710520510

Note: One Terawatt hour is the equivalent of one billion (1 000 million) Kilowatt hours (the Kilowatt hour is the measure that electricity companies use to charge private consumers of electricity).

Source: OECD (2007), *OECD Factbook.*

And education?

- How well do young people balance their lives as learners in school with their lives as consumers? Consumption often offers immediate satisfaction; how does increased consumerism affect learning, as the benefits for learning are often not immediate but lie further in the future?

- Are attitudes towards schooling changing with greater affluence? Do people regard it more as a consumer good than as a public service than in the past?

- What is the role of schools in creating responsible citizens, with civic values and sustainable consumption habits? Should this be the business of schools and teachers at all?

INEQUALITY ON THE RISE

Not everyone benefits equally from economic prosperity. The share of GDP going to people in the form of salaries has been falling while profits have boomed. This creates the conditions for inequalities to widen, even in the affluent OECD countries, when the position of the low skilled becomes ever-more vulnerable while the best-placed high-earners prosper. The general trend since the mid-1980s is towards greater inequality, albeit not everywhere. Trends regarding the position of the top-earners from before 1914 to the present day show signs of a reversal of the pattern of equalisation which lasted until the 1970s. Socio-economic inequality defines an important feature of the broader environment in which schools operate, given that student background is so strongly associated with educational achievement.

Figure 9.3. **Income inequality tending to rise**

Gini coefficients for OECD countries in the mid-1980s and 2000

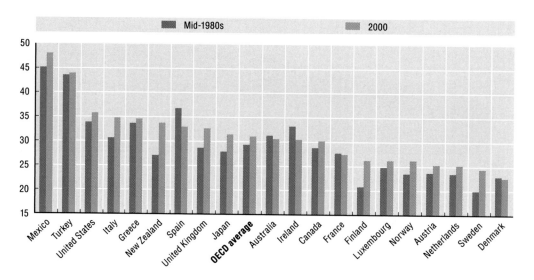

StatLink ᴍᴤ🔳 *http://dx.doi.org/10.1787/404727386160*

Source: OECD (2007), OECD Factbook.

Increasing inequality was found in most OECD countries over the 15 years to 2000. Gini-coefficients offer a summary measure of inequality (expressed as 0 at one end of the spectrum for absolute equality rising with greater inequality to 1 or 100). In the 20 countries permitting comparisons, inequality increased in 16 of them. Northern European countries feature strongly among the most equal, with Mexico, Turkey, the United States and Italy the least.

Other comparisons paint inequality more starkly. The next figure shows long-run trends in the share of total incomes earned by the richest 1 in 1 000 of the population. Before World War II the richest 1 in 1 000 earned 4 to 8% of the total income (in other words their share of income was 40 to 80 times their share of the population). This share fell markedly after World War II and reached levels at around 2% of incomes in the 1960s and 1970s. With the 1980s, the share of income enjoyed by the top 1 in 1 000 income-earners started to go back up again in Canada, the United Kingdom and, especially, the United States: their comparative advantage has gone back up to the levels of the 1920s and 1930s. Not all of the countries share the up-turn, with France and Japan still at 2%.

Poverty levels clearly affect many more people than the privileges enjoyed by the 1 in 1 000 at the other end of the income scale. Nevertheless, the situation regarding the elite is important in shaping wider attitudes and culture, and the priority given to the broad objectives of equity and justice.

Figure 9.4. **The very rich are getting richer**
Income share of the top 0.1% incomes in 5 countries

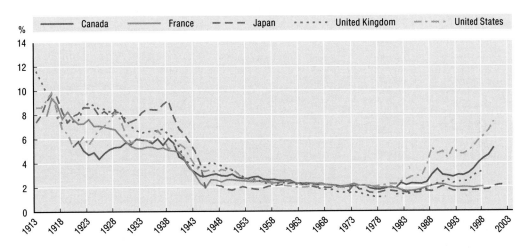

StatLink ▨▨▧ http://dx.doi.org/10.1787/404748728782

Source: OECD (2007), OECD Employment Outlook.

And education?

- Education can stimulate social mobility by providing opportunities but it also helps to reproduce inequalities when the already-privileged have better access to education. Can education be the benefit of all, so that it does not reinforce inequalities?

- Is inequality an inevitable or even desirable part of society? How to balance equity with the legitimate rights of parents to choose what is best for their child?

- Does a more personalised approach to schooling inevitably favour those with the greater cultural resources?

LIFESTYLES WITH HEALTH RISKS

Growing affluence has had a generally positive influence on the health in the OECD countries. People live longer than ever before and are in the main healthier, thanks to such factors as improved living standards, better hygiene, and access to vaccinations and antibiotics. But, with affluence comes new health risks, mostly related to people's own behaviour and habits. Three lifestyle habits with important health effects singled out here are alcohol consumption, smoking and unhealthy eating habits. The picture is a mix of positives and negatives. Research has found that educational attainment is positively associated with healthy behaviour, though the links are complex, while unhealthy lifestyles set new challenges for the educational agenda.

Figure 9.5. **Converging consumption of alcohol across countries**

Litres of alcohol consumption in clustered OECD countries (per capita, aged 15+)

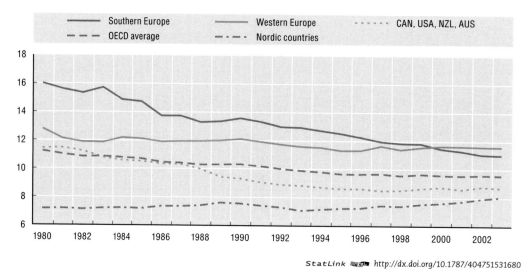

StatLink ⟦═⟧ http://dx.doi.org/10.1787/404751531680

Source: OECD (2005), *Health at a Glance.*

Alcohol consumption has gradually fallen in many OECD countries over the past two decades, albeit at modest rates in recent years, with the biggest drop in the Southern European countries where drinking was highest before. Significant decreases were also seen in the United States, Canada, Australia and New Zealand. Not all share falling alcohol consumption – for example, the Nordic countries (not Denmark), Ireland and the United Kingdom buck the general trend, though it is still lower in the Nordic region than for the other country groups.

Smoking too is on the decline though large disparities remain and it continues to be the largest avoidable risk to health in OECD countries. Beneath the averages are worrying trends for certain sections of our populations, including those nearest to the world of education. The proportion of young women who smoke continues to rise and regular drinking by 15-year-olds considerably increased in many countries in the past ten years, with the most marked increases among girls.

Obesity among children and adults is fast becoming a major public health concern in many OECD countries. It is a known risk factor for several major health problems, including hypertension, diabetes, cardiovascular diseases, asthma, arthritis and some cancers. While we are all on average fatter than twenty years ago, there are very marked differences across countries: more than 1 in 5 have a body-mass index over 30 in the United States, the United Kingdom, Australia and New Zealand, but 1 in 10 or fewer do in the Netherlands, Sweden, Denmark, France, Austria, and Norway, with negligible proportions in Japan.

Widespread obesity suggests significant imbalances between eating habits and physical activity. Taking OECD countries as a whole, estimated daily calorie intake went up by 450 calories per person in the last three decades of the 20th century while sugar consumption has risen by almost 25% since the early 1960s.

Figure 9.6. **Obesity on the rise**

Percentage of people with a body-mass index higher than 30

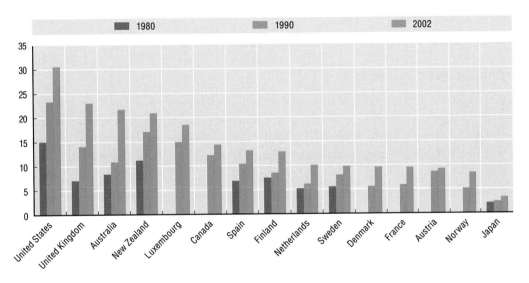

StatLink 🔗 http://dx.doi.org/10.1787/404785003144

Note: Estimates of overweight and obesity rates in most countries are based on self-reported data, but not in Australia, New Zealand, the United Kingdom, and the United States where figures use actual measurement.

Source: OECD (2005), *Health at a Glance.*

And education?

- Is the balance in the curriculum right in ensuring the physical and emotional development of students as well as the cognitive? Do they compete as objectives or do they complement each other as in the adage "a healthy body means a healthy mind"?

- Do schools serve nutritional meals and is sport adequately catered for? What else can be done to improve health without overloading the school curriculum with more and more programmes?

- While smoking and drinking are generally on the decline, they remain important societal problems especially among young people. What are the responsibilities of schools to address these issues, as opposed to families and parents?

FIND OUT MORE

OECD publications used

- OECD (2005), *Health at a Glance*, 2005 Edition, OECD Publishing, Paris.
- OECD (2007), *OECD Factbook*, OECD Publishing, Paris.
- OECD (2007), *Employment Outlook*, 2007 Edition, OECD Publishing, Paris.

Websites used

- WHO Core Health Indicators on-line database: *www.who.int/whosis/database/core/core_select.cfm*.

Related CERI projects

- Social Outcomes of Learning: *www.oecd.org/edu/socialoutcomes*.

Definitions and measurement

- *Gini-coefficient*: A common measure of equality which ranges from 0 in the case of "perfect equality" (each share of the population gets the same share of total income) to 100 in the case of "perfect inequality" (all income goes to the share of the population with the highest income). Household income is adjusted to take account of household size.

- *Alcohol consumption*: Defined as annual sales of pure alcohol in litres per person aged 15 years and over. The methodology to convert alcohol drinks to pure alcohol may differ across countries.

- *Obesity*: Based on the body-mass index (BMI), a single number that evaluates an individual's weight status in relation to height (weight/height^2, with weight in kilograms and height in meters). Based on the WHO current classification, individuals with a BMI between 25 and 30 are defined as overweight and those with a BMI over 30 as obese.

TRENDS SHAPING EDUCATION – ISBN 978-92-64-04661-0 – © OECD 2008